24/7 SAFETY

How to Hybrid 24/7 Safety Leadership Culture

BALASUNDRA K RAJOO

INDIA · SINGAPORE · MALAYSIA

Notion Press

Old No. 38, New No. 6
McNichols Road, Chetpet
Chennai - 600 031

First Published by Notion Press 2019
Copyright © Balasundra K Rajoo 2019
All Rights Reserved.

ISBN

Domestic: 978-1-64587-959-6
International: 978-1-64850-634-5

Dedication

This book is dedicated to the following:

- *My father, Rajoo Kuppan, whom I wish I had the opportunity to spend more years with, especially during my teenage years, to understand him better and for him to see me grow. We miss you, Daddy!*

- *My mom, Marieamal, even though she could not read or write, for continually reinforcing the safety and integrity message; especially at the onset of my working career. We miss you, Mummy!*

- *My wife, Uma, my life partner, and best friend. I would surely be remiss not to give a special note of thanks for the patience and encouragement and for allowing me time and space to get my first book written and published.*

- *Our sons: Vinod Laxmikaanth and Deevak Laxmikaant. Our next generation Industry 4.0; fourth industrial revolution safety leaders. I know it has not been easy for both of you and I do miss the times we could not get together as often as we desired. But, I could not be prouder of the way you both have honored our memories. Both of you are our inspiration, love, and future.*

B-Safe!

```
        H U M I L I T Y
            I N T E G R I T Y
                C O A C H
                C R E D I B I L I T Y
                    T E A M W O R K
    C O L L A B O R A T I O N
                T R U S T
    S E R V A N T H O O D
        C O M M U N I C A T I O N
            R E S P E C T
```

Contents

"Learning to be a progressive 24/7 Safety Leader is a process of watching others and yourself–a lifelong journey."

Preface

This book, *24/7 Safety*, is a snapshot sharing of insights, observations, safety tools, lessons and learnings of how-to hybrid *24/7 SafetyDNA* leadership culture. Its contents are based on my 44 years working safety experience in upstream oil and gas operations. I set out to write about five years ago; sort of a safety reference book for myself; like having your safety friend by your side giving you some practical safety tools, tips, and advice. I am thankful that by jotting down these thoughts and insights into such a safety memory jogger book, it gave me that pause for reference, thoughts, and recollections in my work.

My thought-provoking insights, observations, and reactions shared in this book would hopefully instigate readers to pause, think and act safely and caringly. Having said this, I do understand the practical challenges with individuals' personalities and traits. Why? It's much easier to observe, read, write or speak than it is to embrace or practice it.

It is right to say that a significant fraction of the people out there do not understand what *24/7 SafetyDNA* leadership culture is, or, for that matter, how it looks like and what shape it takes. Why do I say this? People have on numerous instances quizzed me whenever I have shared my thoughts on the subject. Specifically, what does a safety leadership culture look like? My replies have been that it is the consolidated product of people's values, behaviors, habits, beliefs, perceptions, attributes, and personalities that drive commitment or dedication to safety. After listening intently, I have observed people looking blur, tended to scratch their heads and after that, responded, "Sorry, I didn't get that! By the way, even if and when I get it, what shape or form does it take?"

It set me thinking that although those of us who write about safety leadership culture 'might' understand it, the layperson out there on the street does not recognize the intricacies of how this safety culture apparatus looks or works. What a reader needs is concrete, tangible and observable evidence supported by simple safety tools and processes than confusing academic dictionary definitions, stage safety lectures or speeches. How? In essence, the layperson should easily identify observable traits and attributes of safety leadership culture. Thus, my motivation to write this book.

Therefore, this book is crafted to provide the reader with that practical knowledge, practices, tools, and insights required to design, nurture and activate one's *24/7 SafetyDNA*. Additionally, this book captures accounts of leadership practices to spur leadership knowledge. Thus, by consciously writing it down, I hope I can provide some direction to both emerging safety leaders and to refresh those with years of leadership experience. That's what I have endeavored to do in this book.

As said by many of our leaders, **"Everything that happens in our life is not fixated, it can be altered, changed, designed, nurtured and activated or reactivated by constant learning, passion, discipline, and willpower."**

So, here is an opportunity to power up your 24/7 SafetyDNA leadership genetic code!

Acknowledgments

24/7 Safety book has been made possible with the work of many hands. I wish to acknowledge and thank those who shared, participated, contributed and provided me their insights and knowledge.

Each of them can take credit for the success of this book, but none should be held responsible for any errors that may be found in it.

To my work colleagues, co-workers, service and operations contractors, friends, and business partners, special thanks to these people for their help, patience and the many others who have contributed their safety thoughts, safety memories, enouragement and ideas to the completion of the book.

Oil & Gas companies and the people with whom I worked with who launched and set the safety, security and ethical ambience for me. It included ConocoPhillips, ExxonMobil and EnQuest Petroleum drilling, operations and safety managers who provided me the opportunity and taught me about Logistics and Safety, the meaning of servanthood leadership and how to work together in harmony with people of many skills and cultures.

Finally, everyone at Notion Press Publishing for transforming this dream into reality, indeed, I would not have achieved this result without the valuable professional editorial and publishing contributions.

"Safeguarding and protecting people's safety shall be in everyone's best interest for our economy, communities, corporations, fellow workers, friends, and families."

Why Buy This Book?

Thank you for picking up this book. Let's start with a quick bullet list on whether you're looking at the right safety book.

- **Book Structure**: Each insight is about 3–5 pages; each a different insight. It's written for those who typically have little time to read a full safety book.

- **Book Contents**: Starts from a bird's eye (corporate) view and brings it down (floor) to practice and pointers on how to hybrid *24/7 Safety DNA* leadership culture. It is illustrated with controversial views and critiques for debate. Wherever possible, charts, graphs, tables and schematics with simplistic descriptions are used to streamline and deliver key messages.

- **Short and Concise**: It's written in layman's words supported by slogans, and strives to be jargon-free. Its light read, non-statistical, or overly graphic, easy to absorb and apply to your job, home or everyday occurrences in your life. It focuses on basic stuff that matters; and not on academic safety theories.

- **Engages Hearts and Minds**: It offers insights on how to communicate, speak, interact, listen, lead and influence the hearts and minds of your workforce. It charts the path to 'show the real you when no one is watching.'

- **Human Behaviors, Habits and Safe Choices**: Whether you are a new hire, a safety seasoned professional or a long-service company hire, this book encourages you to focus on the way you approach, analyze, lead and manage attitudes, behaviors, habits, personalities, and practices of those working and living with and around you.

- **Do The Right Things:** Shares observations, real-life experiences, learnings, insights, thoughts and core beliefs. Elaborates and lays out how to engage co-workers' mindset to do the right things and make the right safe choices 'even when no one is supervising you.'

- **Safety Culture**: It's written exploring a journey to safety leadership culture. It clarifies that if and when you put safety in your heart (leaders' heart) and at the center of a company (a core value), you can achieve low Incident Frequency Rate or an incident-free culture.

- **Safety Audience**: It's written for all positions, business partners, contractors and company employees. It's aimed at managers and aspiring leaders of multinational corporations, organizations, and enterprises.

- **Safety Guide or Safety Orientation Book:** It would serve as a giveaway for new hires when they report for the first day of work. It's 'a good tool to keep in your toolbox,' travel backpack, office or workstation desk as a quick reference.

So, why wait? If you never turn the pages of this safety book, you will never know what's in store for you. The good news is that if you have made the choice, you are in a position to change lives. Why? Your life itself is like a book.

So, let's get started!

"If we have learned anything from safety incidents of the past, it's that if you don't learn and take the first step to change, you will fail."

Introduction

A Journey Starts With The First Step: Taking The Safety Leadership Culture Journey

Over the last 30 years or so, demographics, technology, safety systems, industrial labor, shortage of knowledge and talented workers and regulatory compliance factors have significantly evolved and impacted our industry safety standards, performances, and workplace culture. This evolution has produced an academically educated, motivated and productive workforce. In some ways, the current workforce work lifestyle's, resources and technology accessible to execute tasks are unrecognizable. What we see today will certainly change and shift in the emerging decades.

What are the visible outcomes of this evolution?

- **Upside:** Safety standards have evolved into a culture of compliance driven by technology, safety, and risk management systems, and regulatory requirements which have raised safety standards, awareness and performance. It has given birth to the culture of safety policy, procedure and regulatory compliance.

- **Downside:** An increase in the severity of large-scale safety incidents, disasters, and failures which have caused loss of lives, property and asset damages, environmental and reputation impacts, adverse corporate financials, and unbearable shareholders losses.

While low consequence safety incidents may have gone unreported or non-investigated, high consequence incidents and disasters such as Bhopal (India), Chernobyl (Russia), Piper Alpha (U.K.), Exxon Valdez (USA), Space Shuttle Challenger (USA), BP Deepwater Horizon (USA) and Fukushima Nuclear Plant (Japan) have received widespread breaking news media coverage.

Every ten years or so, an incident such as this seems to happen. Why? It is not about the 'know-how,' but it is about human nature, integrity, character and corporate attitudes of managers and leaders in charge of risky operations and tasks. Learnings indicate not a single, but a combination of failures such as:

- Profits before safety–decisions were made that saved time and money without full appreciation of the risks involved.

- Not following approved and established procedures.

- Progressively operating assets beyond design life. Companies who are focused on personal safety and not process safety or maintenance of facilities.

- Ignoring incident lessons learned and not executing required changes due to cost pressures.

- Poor quality of safety incident investigations–the management's failure in detecting and intervening early on deteriorating safety standards.

- Poor investigative processes, techniques and a variety of investigators.

- Failed permit to work system; especially the failure to achieve operational controls and maintenance of process systems required by law.

- Miscommunications management or the lack of a reporting and learning culture.

- Competency and training failures, cost-cutting and failure to invest in training, new equipment, and reduced competence across the board.

- Use of defective critical device function testing equipment.

- Inadequate, untrained and tested emergency response and crisis management teams.

- Neglective human performance factors such as fatigue, long shifts, and the poor safety culture.

Sometimes, incidents that hurt us most teach us the greatest lessons in life. Life doesn't provide us the opportunity to go back and fix the past, but it does let us learn and live each next day better than our history. What puzzles the industry leaders and management is that even with shared incident learnings and safety management best practices, why do companies continue to get different results with their safety performances?

Let's review and understand these issues.

1. **Why Different Results**: Safety is policy, procedure and risk systems-driven, and not safety leadership culture-driven.

   - Corporations continue to reduce risk and incidents, and increase operations focused on 'dos and don'ts' without getting down to the roots to understand the operational culture of safety.

   - The focus has been on minimizing the risk of harm on identified risks without structured root cause analysis to uncover relationships between causes and symptoms.

2. **Why Act Now**: Serious hurts, injuries, and fatalities continue to occur as indicated by the 'Evolution of Safety Performance' graph below is of concern such as the lagging indicator Incident Frequency Rate has 'plateaued' over the last decades. Why?

- Despite the best-in-class facilities, infrastructure designs and engineering, high-tech equipment and machinery, strict regulatory legislation, policies and procedures, safety on the ground comes down to people.

- People continue to execute at-risk acts, take shortcuts, make unsafe choices and perform tasks in hazardous conditions.

- Workforce complacency as opportunities, inputs to re-engineer safety of design and infrastructure of facilities have become fewer.

- Automation, digitalization and rogue automated systems at times pose more hazards than rewards.

- Address the fourth industrial revolution with new emerging technology and its associated unknown safety and risk challenges.

- Lower tolerance level among governments, safety regulators and the public on injuries and fatalities.

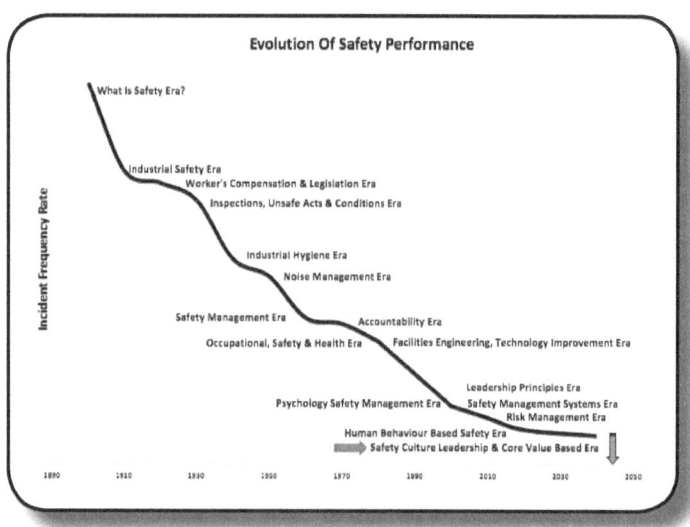

3. **Why This Way:** The current workforce is not there yet regarding **'that's the way we do things around here or it's the way it's done here even when no one is watching.'** I believe that only with this mindset and attitude, corporate management would be able to:

- Create a workforce to make the safe choices.

- Insist on individual leadership to be both the first and last line of defense against hurt, injury, and fatality.

- Nurture, activate and drive, positive, safe choices, actions, and responses.

- Create a safe workplace to be both a personal and a corporate choice.

- Encourage reporting and learning culture. Incidents to be adequately investigated and acted upon.

4. **Who's Responsible:**

1. **Individual:** Exhibit a caring safety culture behavior, and take on a leadership position to ensure safe choices are executed. 'I don't want to see you get hurt' culture.

2. **Team:** Embrace safety as a core value behavior. Speak and report out if they perceive an individual or management behaves, acts or instructs in a manner inconsistent with the safety core vision and values.

3. **Management:** Exhibit executive leadership behavior to monitor and validate the health of the safety culture. How? Engineer and design facilities and infrastructure, roll-out integrity and risk management systems and institute training that mitigate hazards, and eliminate risks or dangers.

5. **Why Change:** Safety performance has plateaued. Therefore, a desire to change is greater than to be the same.

   ▪ Workers taking risks 'when nobody's watching or looking,' is indicative of a concern with the culture of workers or with that organization.

   ▪ Hybrid of safe behavior, options, and ethical conduct is a fundamental foundation to employee-driven safety culture.

6. **What's Next:** For occurrences of incidents or disasters to be avoided, safety must evolve such that individual safety leadership is at the core of safety culture. **Companies must nurture, hybrid and commit to positive human-side safety behaviors and habits so that people demonstrate actions and make safe choices without even being watched, policed or supervised.** How can this be accomplished?

   1. Determine the level at which the safety leadership culture functions

   2. Decide where to take this organizational culture

   3. Chart and navigate a journey to drive down Incident Frequency Rate

7. **What's The Expected Result:** Develop and hybrid a *24/7 SafetyDNA* leadership culture in which the value of safety is embedded in every level and reinforced at every turn, and in every one of the workforces with organizations, enterprises, and corporations.

   ▪ Governments cannot impose and 'police' a company's safety performance or safety culture. Why? Regulators, experts, and safety consultants do provide valuable inputs, additional ad-hoc resources, recommendations and services only. For a corporation to change its culture, change must come from within-management and individuals.

- It's only when individuals as leaders drive safety that you don't have to worry about what they do if or when no one is looking. How? Co-workers and team members will take the leadership role to look out for each other and watch out for non-compliances, unsafe acts, unsafe conditions or behaviors and habits of other workers.

In doing so, the organization's safety journey moves to a transition mode from a 'policy, procedures and risk system rule-driven culture to a core value-safety leadership-based culture.'

The journey to design, nurture and activate such a culture of *24/7 SafetyDNA* leadership is not going to be straight-forward or easy. Why? No matter where we measure ourselves, leadership behaviors, safe choices, and actions are crucial to where we want to be on this journey. It's a journey that must start with you and me.

Now, let's look at the 20 insights in this safety book which can positively drive this change!

"For a culture of safety leadership to design, nurture and activate, don't prioritize it, core value it."

Insight 1

Safety Is Not A Priority. Don't Prioritize It, Core Value It

The Oxford Dictionary defines **safety as 'the condition of being protected from or unlikely to cause danger, risk, or injury' and priority as 'being regarded or treated as more important than others.'**[1] Having defined it, let me say it in a personal tone. Safety is about a person's life–my friend's life, my worker's life, my family's life, and my life. Therefore, where would you position safety with yourself? Would it be a priority or a core value?

Safety should not be something that goes on a policy sheet and then on the corporate walls just for the sake corporate publicity. Safety is to be evolved and nurtured as a core value. If or when people say, "Safety is our top priority," it resonates as a safety language and not protection of the family, care for people and to prevent hurt. Furthermore, it raises another question: how can safety be a priority when it's easy to change against competing needs such as timelines, schedules, cost preferences, budget and production pressures? **For a genuine culture of safety, when there is competition, safety must come out on top every time and not just when it's convenient.**

Here are things to assure you're evolving changes-in direction toward safety as a core value:

- **It Must Be A Personal Core Value:** It must be nurtured over a sustained period where outside influences and demands can't alter. **"Priorities can change; whereas, a core value is deeply rooted as it has engaged one's value."** How do you make it personal?

1. Focus on caring for the individual as a human being

2. Create a culture to capture, learn and share from all incidents both internally and externally

3. Identify and eliminate at-risk behaviors, unsafe choices, conditions and actions proactively

4. Do not overreact when a setback occurs

5. Do not debate 'administrative issues' at the workplace

6. Recognize and celebrate safety milestones along the journey

Just to put it, if safety isn't at the top of your agenda, if it does not start with you, then you probably won't have safety as a personal core value.

Here are several tips on how you can drive this value:

1. You are responsible for your safety first and foremost

2. You must take care of yourself first before you can look after other people

3. You are in control of your actions and choices both safe and unsafe

4. You and only you can make you work safely

5. You are empowered to STOP WORK if or when you encounter an unsafe act or condition

6. Take care of yourself means to take care of your family

7. Personal safety ownership must be with you and not with the management

- **It's An Equally Shared Obligation And Responsibility:** No one individual can do it alone. Everyone is to be held responsible and accountable for what happens Everyone needs to play an equal shared role to keep others, themselves and their workplaces safe. **Being safe and making safe choices shall be the right thing to do not because someone told us to do it, but because it's an obligation, a responsibility, and an expectation!** Safety, therefore, is not a side note, not an option, not just a talk, not just a slogan and not another check marks of one's job description. Instead, safety is a shared core obligation and responsibility expected of all irrespective of position or title.

- **It Requires Commitment At All Levels:** Printed, displayed posters, notices, safety forums, safety workshops, and safety meeting statements that safety is a 'top priority' are commendable and should be encouraged and necessary. However, a show of commitment to safety must run much more.

Here are tactics that can help show commitment:

- Show sincere warmth, caring personal touch, passion, and compassion

- Engage the hearts and minds of people at all levels in the organization—exhibit 'a cultural SafetyDNA leadership commitment'

- Drive and communicate core safety message at every opportunity 'that human life matters, and not getting anyone hurt absolutely matters'

- **It's When Action Speaks Louder Than Words:** The real safety challenge is to translate aspirations into tangible and visible actions. An observation of what's lacking nowadays in safety **isn't just what needs work, what's said or committed; it is often the lack of committed leadership actions to drive safety as a core value.**

Consider how you walk the talk for these examples.

- No mention of safety processes during a production target push or project start-up;

- No reinforcement for positive, safe behavior or safe choices;

- No unsafe actions, conditions or observations reported, discussed or shared;

- No work or updates on reported hazards and dangerous acts

What would be the immediate consequence? What leaders say and share with their workforce gets ignored. Why? Leaders' visible safety behavior and actions contradict with the prescribed core value. As a leader, behavior, actions, and conduct with safety does directly impact your organization's safety standards in totality. After all, safety not being a core value sets up for poor safety standards and places individuals at risk.

- **It's Leadership Reactions, Not Drowned Out Publicity:** Nowadays, safety signs, slogans, directives, alerts, flashes, statements, conditioned and pre-prepared speeches to communicate safety as number one priority have become 'somewhat mundane, repetitive, copied or obsolete, more an art than a science.' Why? **Safety signage and banners are only impactful if what it says is real, tangible, visible and has lived up to through leadership actions on the work level.** If not, it is 'all talk, window dressing, a publicity stunt, carries no substance,' which eventually gets drowned out. The message is that individual safety leadership mindset and safe actions matter.

'Safety is our top priority' sure does sound nice though. Especially the word 'priority.' **Only when there is visible, strong *24/7 SafetyDNA* culture leadership, safety is elevated to be a core value; it's no longer just a priority.**

It is a core value not a priority if and only when:

- It resonates, flourishes with the people;

- It's a value of caring for and engaging of the people;

- It is deeply embedded in the way a company conducts its business;

- Its leadership makes safety crystal clear in their words and actions

Why? Being a core value, one will only commit human life to do their job safely and most importantly, without harm to co-workers and themselves.

"Absolute safety leadership culture transformation can only happen when there is an open, honest, sincere mind, a willing heart, a passion, a caring, and relentless pursuit."

It Start's In The Executive Suites. Triggered At The Top, Measured, And Audited At The Bottom

Over the years, positive vibes with the culture of safety have been noticed in the workforce. "Oh yes, we've come a long, long way." Those were the days when the workforce compiled, no matter what was said and thrown at us without detailed scrutiny. With greater emphasis from regulators, governments and the public, most companies' lagging indicator has gone to low Incident Frequency Rate. Furthermore, corporate safety strategy nowadays is strategized toward an incident-free culture focused on high-tech engineering and ergonomic designs and infrastructure, risk and integrity management systems, behavioral leadership practices, styles and safety best practices!

Success, in some ways, is credited to those from corporate suites where the strategic focus has been to:

- Implement and steward a sustained and sound organizational safety culture;

- Cascade safety leadership as a line responsibility down organization levels;

- Delegate safety best practices as an integral part of the line leadership, rather than the sole domain of safety officers, safety managers or safety departments;

- Streamline and optimize safety, risk management, and control systems through effective safety leadership and workers partnership

A corporation's safety policy is seen as a commitment from the ivory corporate towers. Ironically, even though such responsibility gets 'triggered' at the top, reaching the bottom has not been an easy task, let alone a smooth ride. Even if this may be the case, it has not uniformly translated into practical applications. Moreover, it is even more apparent when the safety tone from the top gets diffused or lacks visible executive leadership actions. For example, while safety messages, directives and policies may read 'safety first,' when it gets co-mingled with production priorities, then people perceive production to take precedence over safety.

Some say management executives can only invoke authority and less about influence over the workforce. Let's consider the following pointers:

- **First Understand What's Your Organization's Safety Culture:** The 'Safety Culture' phrase is widely defined across the industry but rarely understood. The U.K. Health and Safety Commission defines safety culture as follows: **"The product of individual and group values, attitudes, perceptions, competencies, and patterns of behavior that determine the commitment to, the style and proficiency of, an organization's health and safety management."**[2]

Every corporation, company, enterprise or organization has some common internal personalities and characteristics. The paradox is that it is only invisible to insiders, but not to outsiders. How do you identify these characteristics? The safety culture in an organization is its behavioral expectations, practices, and norms which can be identified and observed when people are queried. The resultant responses could be as follows:

1. "What's in it for me with safety?"

2. "Who cares as long as you don't get hurt?"

3. "Safety is only an issue if or when an incident happens."

4. "Safety is managed by policy, procedures, and documentation."

5. "Safety is managed by workforce training, coaching, involvement, and engagement."

6. "Safety is how the business operates and runs here."

7. "Safety is the real you when no one is watching."

- **Safety First For Me:** Traditionally, once grassroots have absorbed 'safety first for me,' with corporative executives, it is no longer an executive process. It is an embedded 24/7 safety culture within the organization. To make this transformation or shift, company executives need to design, nurture and activate a *24/7 Safety DNA* mindset and drive safety tone from the top and progressively foster grassroots ownership. Consider the following in your daily grind:

  1. Shift behaviors, habits, beliefs, and values to underpin and drive the organization's *24/7 Safety DNA* leadership.

  2. Influence safety leadership development and training to demonstrate and enhance safety qualities.

  3. Set the tone for emerging safety leaders and followers to seek high standards of safety culture. Why? People will follow leaders' example more than advice.

  4. Culture transformation and implementation of procedures and policies need to be done WITH people and not TO people. Why? We get educated on the right safety behavior in policies/procedures and thereafter understand the transformation being implemented.

- **Accountability First For Me:** Safety accountability does place the greatest challenge on front-line workers who have the least control and the highest probability of getting hurt. In some cases, a lack of accountability is observed when executives, despite fancy titles and positions, don't seem to know or understand what's going on, don't get much done and don't 'walk the floor or walk the talk.'

It is crucial that executives from the top display a positive safety personal accountability. Why? If safety is not an executive's accountability, it will take a natural tumble to the bottom of the priority list with grassroots.

- Accountability starts with everyone–you and me, and it helps if and when it is seen driven from the top (executives in corporations);

- Instill accountability on the front end of interactions (forums, seminars workshops, and toolbox meetings) in their corporate strategy to establish and drive the right direction and impetus;

- Front-corporate loaded accountability breeds better relationships, eliminates surprises, improves confidence, collaboration, job satisfaction, and after that, it drives safety performance to the next bar.

Once people have embraced personal accountability, then improvement in workforce morale is a natural by-product of the *24/7 SafetyDNA*.

- **Safety Metrics:** The organization's safety culture needs to be one that is open, measurable and transparent. It has to be one that proactively reports all incidents including minor and near misses and hits or hurts. In this process, consider the following:

  1. **Corporate executives must drown people's perception that safety is all about statistics and metrics a 'numbers game'**; as it's an obstacle to achieving safety vision and values

  2. **Companies who perform world-class in safety don't just talk about lagging, leading and personal indicator statistics or allow safety metrics to drive safety culture; instead, they use *24/7 SafetyDNA* culture to drive metrics.**

- **Safety Statistics Analytics:** Generally in corporations, safety statistics are painstakingly harvested at the bottom, compiled, analyzed, measured and audited at the middle and presented and reported at the top. Thereafter, safety strategies for continuous improvements, initiatives, refresher training, and tools are introduced so that actions and not for managing statistics.

With regards to safety statistics, here are the ways to get executive attention:

1. Analytics shall be clear and meaningful, explains what it reflects; one which avoids statistical jargon and spells out risks.

2. Deliver the facts, and honor CEOs position, knowledge, experience, skills and own senses with trust.

3. Trust but verify; don't 'assume' CEOs who read technical terms, jargons and statistics understand what they mean.

4. Analytics should be simple, neatly presented in an organized fashion and described in a compelling format.

5. Do not 'manufacture' incident and injury, lagging and leading indicator spreadsheets and data, graphs and colorful power point charts that provide little or no actual or factual value concerning incident and injury prevention.

6. Leadership must be able to identify risks and provide inputs and feedback to implement enhanced safety programs to remedy issues and concerns.

Companies who aspire for healthy and nurtured *24/7 Safety DNA* mindset must set the tone from the top and foster bottom-up safety ownership. Therefore, unflinching support and guidance from top corporate executives is an essential ingredient in making it happen with getting triggered at the top, actions executed, results measured and audited at the bottom.

"A culture of safety is composed of life experiences influenced by balanced safety risk decision making, authority, leadership, and strategic execution."

Insight 3

"Don't Fall For The Sucker's Choice." Safety Versus Production, Safety Is A Cost; Not An Investment

Corporations do establish safety, health, environment, security and ethics policies. Thereafter, compliance is sought. At times, this expectation does not get translated into practice as it trickles down the organization's hierarchy levels.

Have you heard of these expressions or statements?

- "At times, I feel like safety takes the number one priority when it suits management."

- "Safety seems to get management's attention right after an incident."

- "Management is here again for another safety day field trip! It's likely another of those rah-rah safety speeches."

- "A company only cares about meeting production volumes and targets, on-time venture or project execution against milestones, and all of these are to be accomplished below the set budget."

Such perceived conflicts and thoughts are challenging ones to be addressed. Having said this, it is the corporation's leadership with ultimate responsibility and accountability to seek and resolve such perceptions and conflicts.

Here are some thoughts to make consensus building work for you:

- **Making Right Safe Choices:** Have you heard of these justifications?

  - "We don't have the time to meet for a safety toolbox meeting, attend safety workshops, safety training, safety chats or safety talks as we have other critical tasks to be addressed."

  - "We need to allocate manpower resources and budgets to meet our production volumes and project targets as a priority, and not safety."

  - "We do not have the staffing to work on safety hazard hunts, unsafe observations, risk assessments or to participate in any incident investigations."

  - "We do not have the safety budget to implement safety initiatives as suggested by the corporation's safety department."

Whatever said and done, employees and managers are continuously challenged with making choices through consensus to achieve the following:

- Do the safe-productive things

- Balance priority clashes between safety and production

- Weigh options for a balanced integration of safety and production priorities

- **Safety Culture Change Resistance:** Safety culture gives every group and organization its unique identity. How? It can either be positive, "I know that the people I work with will do nothing to jeopardize my safety," or negative, "All management cares about is production numbers and profits, and safety is damned." **Entrenched assumptions, whether accurate or inaccurate, influence the behavior and attitudes of group members. Once ingrained, culture is highly resistant to change.**[3]

Make no mistake. The way someone thinks about safety and its balanced, safe choices impacts how he or she would execute their job. Corporations' leaders' duties and responsibilities, therefore, need to be tied to how to manage such resistant behaviors. Why? If people are in the resistant mode, they will forever remain trapped in the illusion that safety programs and systems are pointless, obstructive or executive propaganda.

- **Safety Seen Not As An Investment:** Here are a couple of pointers on how this conflicting thought defers with the company's desired safety results:

    - **Companies with world-class safety performance have low total recordable incident frequency rate, are efficient, productive, tend to be long-term focused and have a healthy shareholder bottom line.** Such companies have deep-rooted safety cultures and perceive resources investment into safety as a long-term investment and not as an increased financial cost or expenditure.

    - **Companies with low or mediocre budget and manpower allocations for safety tend to be short-term focused, and they do not deem financial safety expenditures as an investment into safety or as a necessity.** Such companies are inclined to 'siphon' or reallocate safety budgets to increase production volumes through new technologies, research, and development, exploration, acquire new production acreage and farm operating licenses to generate more profit for shareholders.

Safety does generate profits in corporations with world-class comprehensive integrity and risk management systems–ones who have devoted resources effectively to implement and steward such tools. Such corporations, therefore, tend to take sound assessed risks that others dare not. **"What creates incidents and financial cost is not safety,** but bad safety management." Once the management realizes that safety is financially rewarding with positive returns, then the road to safety excellence is open. **Investment for safety is an investment in care for the people.** It is far-reaching than financial savings or profits.

- **Safety, Cost, And Investment:** With most companies, executive leadership responsibilities are chartered to meet these strategic objectives:

  1. Reduce lost-time Incident Frequency Rate and recordable injuries

  2. Implement and steward a safety culture-focused methodology, risk and integrity management systems and sound safety training tools

  3. Safety and production performance priorities are addressed equally as operating cost and product quality

  4. Increased return on investment for shareholder

- **Risk Management And Regulatory Compliance**: Proactive risk mitigation and reduction is recognized as a pillar of safety culture excellence among the high-risk energy sector (e.g., oil and gas or nuclear) is no exception as it poses a great risk if not the greatest! Why be proactive?

  1. Companies that do identify and manage risk tend to outperform others and concurrently decrease the likelihood of incidents, bad reputation, asset damage, fines, litigation and even share price drop.

  2. Companies focused on 'getting it executed right the first time, every time' do emerge successful, profitable, reputable and a sustainable operating business.

Anytime, workers perform anything in a company or organization, there is an element of risk involved; in fact, "everything we do–from

the moment we're born–carries an element of risk, and his survival depends on how well he manages those risks."[4]

What are some notable observations, behaviors, and characteristics of corporations when challenged to maximize profits:

- Perceive risk management, regulatory and compliance requirements as 'constraints imposed by the rule of law.'

- Aspire a sustained and uninterrupted production with short-term gains

- Reap profits through maximum production at the lowest operating cost

- Skip safety risk assessments in a rushed start-up of new plants, operating facilities or acquired assets

- Allow design errors not to be identified or corrected prior to operations start-up

- No risk assessments are conducted in the transition from project to operations phase

- Mandate or authority to STOP WORK to field site operators is not delegated due to corporate policy delegation bureaucracy.

- **Safety Goals Versus Production Goals:** The critical question is, do safety and production priorities ever coexist? Production is tailored for the company's profitability and growth, whereas, safety is designed to protect people, environment, asset integrity, corporation reputation and security. So, if the aim is to improve, maximize profits and grow the corporation, then both 'technically' have the same goals and priorities. Therefore, **safety is not to be construed as an obstacle or hindrance, but rather a 'catalyst' to expedite production volumes and**

targets safely. Thus, an organization's operating culture of safety and production volumes is not to be differentiated as it creates an impression of an existing imbalance between safety and production.

Safety and production both, are critical for any company's continuity, sustainability, and profitability. I think, finding the right balance between safety and production priorities determines the success of the industries.

"24/7 SafetyDNA leadership transformation happens when there is relentless safety learning, sharing, engagement and execution of safe choices and actions by the people, of the people and for the people."

Insight 4

It Is People; It Is People, It Is People

People are the face of any organization as they are the greatest, most valuable asset and obviously the critical solution to the safety culture excellence puzzle. **A company's safety is only as proper as the safety of the people that work for it.** It is people's safety that matters, and it is protected at all times. Managing a culture of safety to many from the outside world may seem natural–make sure people don't get hurt!

Although you've implemented the world's most significant safety programs and best practices, given the most significant training, if the people don't believe it, can't embrace it, don't agree with its leadership and don't drive the culture of safety, then you don't have one!

Globally, company leadership manages safety 24/7 covering these five pillars:

- No. 1: **P**–Safety and care of their **people.**

- No. 2: **E**–Protect the **environment.**

- No. 3: **A**–Protect the **asset.**

- No. 4: **R**–Safeguard the company's **reputation.**

- No. 5: **S**–Protect and secure people and company's asset **security.**

It's traditionally noted that if leadership takes care of No.1, people take care of the rest. It's as simple as that. 'Take care of your people, and they'll certainly take care of the company.' **In practice, to achieve a**

safe organization; more a sustained safety performance, its only possible with the commitment of the people and its leadership. Why? People are the most significant variable piece of the puzzle in any corporation's safety performance.

Here are a couple of techniques to accomplish great things with safety through people:

- **People's Passion Drives Culture:** Safety leadership transformation starts with people (you and me), at our homes, in our backyards, offices and field sites.

  - People come-and-go including executives. Therefore, pursue to build loyalty with passion, and care to ride a journey that ultimately outlasts all of us.

  - People have an inner desire to be a part of something bigger, grander and dream of safety excellence milestones, awards or recognition.

  - People can only energize and motivate up so much.

  - People want to be noticed and recognized for their work–they want to remain relevant, search for new ways to learn, improve their skills and invest in themselves.

  - People know big moments are rare, and want to aspire and get attached to a vision and a core value to make it a reality.

  - People with the best ideas are most effective in follow-ups.

  - People desire to feel essential–to see their ideas, efforts, and contributions had produced something significant.

- **People Management:** Working safely is a condition of employment. Having the right people is more important than having proper policies and procedures. In the hiring and interview screening, implement and look for the following:

- Attract, recruit and hire the right best-talented people

- Hire people with the same shared safety core values as the organization

- Train, coach, mentor and retain *24/7 Safety DNA* mindset individuals

- Hybrid new hires with the right safety choices skillsets from the onset

- Communicate that safety is a condition of employment prior to the hire

- Encourage people to have 24/7 safety conversations

- Hire people who exhibit attitudes and attributes to succeed as Safety Champions

- Breed and inject habits that 'no work is to be performed if it is not performed safely'

- Hire people that complement your and the corporation's strengths.

As said by Aristotle, **"We are what we repeatedly do; excellence, then, is not an act but a habit."**[5] Hybrid and repeatedly implant safe behavior, habits and attitudes into people's conscious decisions regardless of the people's position, title, the color of the coveralls or work clothes. People, when hired, assume different positions, titles, and roles. After that, everyone is part of the team, and everyone's contribution is critical to the corporation's safety success.

- **Ignite Hunger, Proving Others Wrong:** Show care, ignite safety hunger and drive people to overachieve and take responsible, safe actions as follows:

  - Embrace, breed and hybrid 'outside-the-box' safety thinking.

- Never underestimate people's ability to perform until you have evaluated and tested their potential *24/7 Safety DNA*.

- Sustain high levels of motivation, open doors of opportunity and accelerate their chances for advancement.

- Guide and push them to get there. How? Allocate majority of your time and attention on the 20% of your people that generate 80% of your safety excellence results.

- Share your journey with people–failures, adventures, and successes. Why? Sometimes, we fall, we break and we fail, but we must then rise, heal and overcome.

- Motivate people. Give them perspectives on how to achieve safety excellence.

- Create opportunities to leave a long-lasting legacy that rewards the organization, the people we serve and for future generations to learn.

- **People's Happiness:** Happy employees are safe and productive employees. **Happiness is found in people who live and speak kindly, care profoundly and give time and effort generously.** At times, leaders are victims of taking their work too seriously. As leaders, do step back, enjoy the journey, forget your happiness and create happiness for others. Happiness can be evidenced when people start to share expressions as follows:

  - My company wants me home safe so that I can hug my loved ones

  - My life is a gift from God. It's irreplaceable

  - My company does not put my well-being and safety at-risk while at work

  - My company does not permit us to cut corners and take at-risk actions to meet production targets or volumes

- My job starts every day with me taking notice of the Safety Countdown Board–'Safety Begins And Starts With Me Here.'

- My task every work day is to put my signature without fail on the Zero Safety Incident Board as a daily safety reminder, a step back for caution while at work and as a source of safety pride

- We are happy, motivated, recognized and rewarded for operating without an incident every day

We often think that when things change, people will be happy, but the truth is when people are happy things will change, and people will accept change. Therefore happiness is a choice, not a result.

- **People Demand Respect**: Treat people with respect regardless of their job, position or title. **The goal of any leader isn't to be liked or loved; it's to be respected by his or her people.** Be an accurate reflection of a person of what you'd like to be remembered. If you want love, give love. If you want the truth, be truthful. If you want respect, give respect to receive the respect.

   Get to know your people, meet them, go down to the floor where they are working. **People are the heart of a business. It is the people who walk the extra mile to make it happen or not be an obstacle and stop it from happening.** Why? When people feel respected, informed and included in the safety decision-making process, people will participate, start to communicate and feel safe about the organization for which they work.

- **'Us Versus Them' Mentality:** Motivated people are the foundation of success for a company today and in the future. Do not create an 'us versus them' mentality as it won't help achieve set goals and strategic objectives. How? Command an influential

24/7 Safety DNA culture and be a beacon of leadership, hope, and inspiration. Eliminate us versus them mentality regardless of differences in titles, positions, where you show up on the organization chart, pay scales or job responsibilities.

Take time to invest in your people who helped make your organization what it is today. Why? **Without people's support and without the spirit of working together, safety success is not entirely possible.** Be reminded that the irreplaceable person behind every injury statistics helped you prioritize your safe choices and actions, and that people are partners in safety and not your adversaries.

- **Know People's Basic Safety Rights:** It's what people should know and choose to live by choice and not by chance, to make changes and not excuses.

Here are examples of peoples' fundamental safety rights:

- To be aware of potential risks, existing hazards, and unsafe conditions prior to the commencement of work.

- To actively participate in hazard hunt programs.

- To be directed to report-out unsafe observations, acts, and conditions.

- To refuse hazardous practice or to work in dangerous situations.

- To be brave, have courage, guts, and demand management mandate to STOP WORK, call a time-out and tell the management.

- To STOP WORK when it is not safe to continue or when not sure.

- To be able to raise the hand, speak up and ask questions when not sure.

- Corporate management is obligated to inform people of their rights, document such communications and share it company-wide.

- People need to be told, have their voices heard, protected and recognized for their contribution to safety decisions including the power to stop a job if it can't be done safely. "A job is done well only when it is done safely."

- For those who continue to seek harm, take unsafe choices, take on at-risk tasks or don't work safe, the message should be, "You are not welcomed here."

- Reinforce safe choices, behaviors, and habits.

- Encourage people to identify hazards.

- Promote the need to intervene voluntarily if and when necessary.

- **Organization Structure, Processes, And Culture:** An organizational culture that does not allow the opportunity to express yourself, to listen, to grow, or to be heard, one that lacks feedback mechanism and with layered levels to review to confirm simple decisions is an organization with unattainable and unrealistic goals. Unstructured processes do not support workplace flexibility and safety. Why? It encourages people attritions due to frustrations of wasted time in reviews and meetings, non-productive use of resources and suffocates people's career growth opportunities.

To keep it simple, the graphical bar chart illustration of the "Safety Journey Where Are We?" with people can be related. Our safety journey is now at a juncture with a need to design, nurture and activate Safety Culture Leadership in people with human behavior as a foundation to further drive down the Incident Frequency Rate.

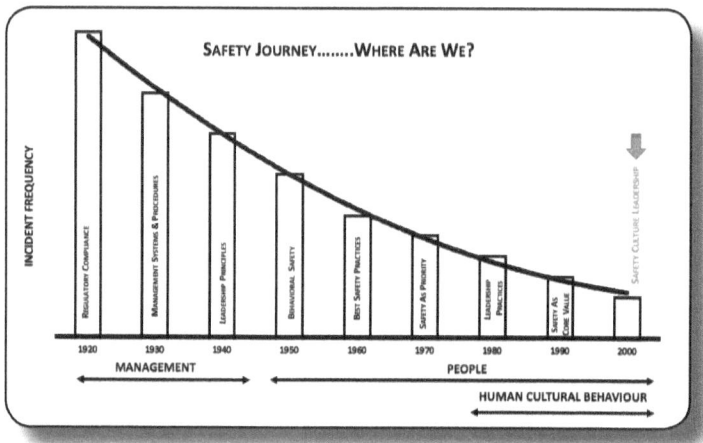

It's a long journey–let's focus, hybrid and continue learning and sharing. To recap what it has taught me and what we have learned:

1. It's about people. Most critically, it's about people safety; it's about lives.

2. It's people's *24/7 Safety DNA* that drives people's behavior and habits. After that, such behavior hybrids and inspires the culture of safety.

3. Treat people as fellow human beings, and not some people in the corporate machinery.

4. Things that you do for yourself are gone when you are gone, but things you do for people remain as your legacy.

5. Deal with people holistically–a sum of parts that include work, family, relationships, and emotions.

6. Engage people with the care that they matter to you at work and life.

7. People genuinely do not decide or have control over their future. They choose and absorb behaviors; as such, they tend to drive their prospects.

"People must have their say—not get used to saying 'it is what it is.' It's that if you don't show up, if you don't speak up and if you don't ask everyone else, you will eventually fail."

Insight 5

Don't Ask Top Management, Ask Everyone Else

What people communicate, share, express and what they talk about with regards to safety is the pulsating heartbeat of a company's safety culture. If you want to assess the perception and health of safety within a company as manifested in people's behaviors, habits, attitudes, personalities, and aspirations, then don't ask top management; question everyone else. Pay attention to feedback shared from water cooler and pantry conversations, around locker rooms, washrooms, during work, coffee or lunch breaks and in cafeterias or hallways.

Why? It is imperative that the management is abreast of safety concerns to address them before small issues become significant detractors. How to do this? Don't just ask the management, but ask everyone else too. Why? With rapidly changing and robust organizations with safety, you have to count on the grassroots feedback who form the majority of a company's population–the frontline with work execution.

- **Why Ask Everyone Else:**
  - **Relationship Building**: Seek knowledge, show you care, raise self-esteem, obtain feedback and build credibility and trust. Why? **A company doesn't evolve or behave in a certain way unless every single employee or contractor is involved, energized and acknowledges that safety is all about human life**

- **Measure Company's Safety Journey**: Managers need to to gauge, measure and evaluate the intensity of feedbacks, responses, and answers received from their grassroots workforce to fully understand the status of the company's safety journey.

- **How To Ask:**

  - Try gentle questioning versus passing down an order or directive in the form of "Do it this way, all right, my way!" How? Make it known that they are assured the security that they will not be punished or criticized for being open and truthful in sharing their safety concerns.

  - Use resources such as simple electronic surveys, suggestion boxes and emails which are sufficient and cost-effective if it's not possible to ask questions with face-to-face interactions, especially, for those in remote worksites.

  - Be real and start with an open-ended and non-defensive question: Did you know? How could this have happened? Ask your staff to update you on their safety issues and challenges regardless of the answers.

  - Make honest, sincere, and timely attempts to respond. Why? It results in improved employee morale, productivity and drives the safety performance bar up a few notches.

  - Build trust first and foremost. How? Get to know your people by their first name to give a feeling that they are noticed.

  - Listen well, and allow people to speak up and share first. After that, understand what people say and why they said it. You don't have to agree to everything that's said, and if you don't, explain and clarify why. **"With safety and security discussion issues, disagreement does not mean disrespect."**

  - Sincerely and intently listen to feedback. **Do not listen to respond, but listen to understand**. Why? People seek and approach leaders for support and trust that you will hear and assist wherever possible. Listen up, build morale and not destroy. How? Pay attention and listen to what employees have to say and respond, revert and resolve issues timely.

- Criticize people constructively, especially, in open forums, seminars, and gatherings. Give praise, recognition and celebrate success when it's due to the people. Most importantly, do it promptly.

- Be energized, kind, compassionate and content, but don't stop questioning and improving safety. How? Always speak the truth to the power, and show a passion for the relentless pursuit of safety excellence.

- Employees thoughts and opinions are to be valued. How? Create a 24/7 atmosphere where freedom of questioning and expression is encouraged, "no all yes man team." A 'team of rivals' is required who will speak up for safety–call-out actions that do not seem to comply with 24/7 SafetyDNA core values.

- **What Results Do We Get When Asked:** Usually when you ask, people's feedback can be bucketed into three hierarchy levels:

  - **Upper Management**–Being on the corporate organization chart, executives generally tend to be optimistic about the company's safety culture, its associated safety, and risk management programs and level of safety performance. Why? After all, it's the upper management who are tasked to develop the strategic safety goals, verify and validate its execution status and cost and manage and deploy resources. So, in their minds, it must be working well.

  - **Middle Management**–Mid-level managers' views tend to be practical–ones who will willingly share critical feedback and an assessment on the actual implementation, status of safety programs, outcomes of safety audit results, state and health of their integrity and risk management systems and its current incident frequency trends or rates

- **Workers**–Now, when you get down to field workers, irrespective of whether employees or contractors, they'll tell you what happens from their hearts and minds as they experience it and as they see it.

Therefore, it's not the upper management who indeed are the only ones knowledgeable enough to give you real-time safety performance feedback and assessment. Unfortunately, the majority of executives believe they have deep insights, knowledge and all the answers even though they know that they couldn't possibly know everything that's going on the ground. Why? Being executives, it is ingrained in their DNA to have 'all the right answers, all the right solutions, all the time.' Many put on a brave face and pretend to know particularly when a direct-report or when a peer poses them questions to look good and want to seem 'to be on top of things.'

Experience tells us that the people on the floor are the ones who have specific information to improve and give you a pulse of an organization's safety status and culture.

- **How Do You Do It:** Go out to the floor and ask for their involvement and feedback. Don't wait for it to come to you or for it to happen. Actively investigate opportunities to involve everyone about their safety at work. How? Get personal, ask about safety, life goals and how to reach those goals. It's not enough to tell workers that safety comes first–if that were the case, the safety first signs would be all you need.

  - **Workers:** Learn, understand and share how consequences of front line's and grassroots' unsafe choices and actions, and how subsequent incidents can impact the things they value most.

- **Union:** Involve and seek union members to comply with the provisions of the Employment Act. Why? Unions do make a difference to help change and expedite the growth of the safety culture within an organization. How? With grassroots feedback and involvement, unions tend to help heal the strains between management and workers, and they offer a common goal that everyone could accept.

- **Management:** Support, but don't dominate. How? Start every toolbox operations meeting, workshop and a seminar with a Safety Share. Talk directly to the audience, keep it brief, stay positive and engaged, demonstrate your points clearly and if possible, tell a story and not a statistic. Get everyone on the same page and vision. Seek out 'unforced safety errors.' Make everyone understand that safety has no hidden agendas and no gotchas.

24/7 SafetyDNA **leadership happens by choice, and so do incidents.** Every individual's feedback and input is critical and necessary to make a difference in the enhancement of safety culture. It's not something that should happen to you. It's something that you are part of–that's an important distinction when you're driving a positive *24/7 Safety DNA* culture.

So, when looking for input and feedback, don't just look up the organization chart, but also look left, right and center, but most certainly, look down. Don't only ask or question top management. A high starting point and the 'best barometer' to assess safety, is to ask everyone else.

"Speak from the heart, engage the mind, speak passionately and share the safety journey in ways that appeal to people."

"Engage The Hearts And Minds." Speak From The Heart, And Speak With Passion

Communicate, communicate and communicate. So far, I have not heard complaints about leaders overexpressing or over-communicating. On the contrary, claims are about a lack of communication. **Communication is absolutely critical. It is an 'invincible human voice bridge,' a connection to bind and bond cultures and weave organizations.** A little communication goes a long way. It's simple but important. Why? Communication is the human emotional bonds to excite people to hear, to get to know people, to seek feedback and to get things done. Sometimes, the greatest adventure in our life is to have a heartfelt conversation with someone or some people. Seeking employees or leaders with good communications skills is a major challenge for companies now.

Communicating about safety fosters a sincere sense of passion for keeping people safe at work. Paul O' Neill, CEO of Alcoa said, **"A great safety speech isn't about yelling orders and telling staff to improve safety and completely change their thinking or else. Instead, it's a unique opportunity–a moment of time to motivate staff to work together and have open communications from the CEO down, and unite for the common good of the group."[6]**

- **Why Safety Communication Matters:** Create a conducive, people-friendly environment to hear what people have to say, express concerns, ideas to be heard, and after that, promote connection, collaboration, and relationship building.

Without communication, there is no relationship. With safety, always stay upbeat with communications! How? Such things do not happen spontaneously; it requires organizations to pump up the pulse, and it's 24/7 leadership driven. It must come from the inside-out with passion and at times, with compassion and love.

The advent of the digital age has changed the way and speed with which we communicate. With social media applications like WhatsApp, Facebook, Twitter, etc., we can now record and share our thoughts and opinions to a much larger audience than with the traditional face-to-face chats.

Here are some techniques you can use to inspire and reach out to the people:

- **Safety From The Get Go!:**
  - Incorporate health and safety expectations in your selection, assessment and evaluation hiring criteria and communicate
  - Recruit only people with everyday shared health and *24/7 Safety DNA* attitudes and mindset during interviews. Communicate why such individual(s) were recruited
  - Communicate health and safety policies and expectations before you sign-off the employment offer
  - Get a department or safety manager to communicate safety expectations and policies to new starters during the New Hire Orientation Program to drive messages
  - Use round tables and no formal dress code to reinforce team concept, availability, and flexibility during new hires' orientation sessions.

- **Written And Electronic Communications:** Safety communications are to be transmitted to all inclusive of those operating in remote and geographical sites concurrently. How?

- Research and execute the most expeditious and cost-effective process to communicate. How? Harness and capitalize on information cyber technology resources, and communicate freely over secured networks.

- Keep the writing simple, accurate and easy to be understood

- Managers who communicate by email, texting, and websites need to know their target audience. Why? Readers cannot read communicators' facial expression or hear the tone of their voice.

- Create a concise, upbeat and inspiring safety vision statement. How? Get the senior management to sign, share and display at all operating sites

- Traditional static text posters, bulletins, and messages on walls lack the impact as compared to one displayed on digital screens. How? It captures the audience instantly to convey emergency procedures and real-time safety indicators through video, audio, graphical and text-based content.

- Implement digital communication which is centrally controlled through a multi-device network. Why? It delivers 24/7 safety information and indicators live with real-time updates, coverage and 'breaking safety and security news.'

- Adapt to virtual reality in the way people communicate, meet and interact. How? Master various media using multiple platforms

- **Engage, Capture Hearts And Minds:** Safety communications should be a personal decision for leaders and not one that gets mandated to do. Why? It's an avenue for leaders to display integrity, honesty, trust and a courage voice and seek the workforce to buy into the core value–safe operation is a natural and cultural way to conduct business.

Here are a couple of pointers for consideration:

- Do share where and when people did the job safely and made the right safe choices and decisions to put safety first

- Talk about what worked and the potential harm people prevented proactively. Why? It adds excellent positive recognition and a personal touch

- Communicate people's efforts to resolve safety issues either while on the work floor or during safety meetings or workforce forums. Why? If participation or contribution goes unnoticed or unappreciated, people's enthusiasm toward safety fades, and after that, it turns to cynicism.

- Identify and share key safety initiatives and best practices people have executed to mitigate risks. How? Point out successes of someone else on your team that promoted safe behaviors and choices

- **Presenters And Speakers**: Presenters should not show up with some last-minute pencil-whipped materials to read safety points text off presentation slides. Instead, they should lead a two-way safety communication. Why? Such delivery lacks passion as it portrays the presenter as unprepared and directed, and not because the presenter valued it. **Safety communication shall be a two-way street to communicate and share safety future destination in ways that attract and appeal to people.**

- **Speak From Your Heart:** Communication is to be delivered with sincere intentions from the heart with care for people. **Build people support from the outside-in, and speak core values around safety at work from the inside-out.**

Try the following tips:

- Tap into something passionate and authentic, and leave your audience forever changed. Why? Listeners value authenticity and do sniff out the fake news and mundane messages

- Share personal experiences and memories with sincerity and honesty

- Get a sense of what you want to say and what the people want to hear

- Speak passionately from the heart. Why? It allows people to listen, sense and evaluate who and what you're, and endorses why they should listen to you

- Build a caring relationship when conveying a message. It doesn't require a big talk! A soft word is enough! Why? It's not the 'mouth' that speaks! It's the 'heart' that 'feels'

- Go from conveying content to connecting emotionally and compelling, safe choices and actions. How? Encourage workers to thank each other for using approved and established safe work practices.

- Recognize that some in the audience may not like what you said, but you have a right to say it without needing to justify it. Why? Saying it sincerely and from the heart is the right thing to do

- **Internalize Communications, Listen As You Speak: "People who speak from the heart, listen with their heart."**

  - Authentic listening increases the power of influence over the workforce. Covey captures it well in Habit 5–most people do not listen with the intent to understand; they listen with the intent to reply. Why? People, when they talk, repeat what they know. However, if you hear as you speak, you learn something new to ensure previous mistakes don't get repeated.

- Practice humility. Why? Humility it's being honest about your weaknesses. No one individual has all the right answers. Always be aware that you are not the most intelligent and knowledgeable person in the room at all times.

- As you speak, tune into what is happening at the moment. Why? Listen for thoughts. Understand what ticks and what's essential to capture buy-in.

- Observe and take notice of nonverbal cues–a smile, a light touch on the hand, raised eyebrows and hand under a chin, Why? Facial and bodily expressions and movements show audience reactions.

- Recognize that everyone has gifts and talents. Do not kill talent. Listen to everyone, and learn from everyone. Why? "Nobody knows everything, but everyone knows something."

- Choose to respond without defending and to speak without offending. How? Do it only after the speaker has vented his or her thoughts. Why? It allows the speaker to listen to his or her inner voice and own instincts.

- Say what you need to say from your heart and in your mind!

- **Audience Connection: "Speak in a way that others love to listen to you. Similarly, listen in such a way that others love to speak to you."**

Try the following techniques:

- Compel the audience to be alert, engaged and awake. Why? You have many different personalities and characters in your organization. Don't assume that you can manage everyone the same way, and don't assume everyone likes to be handled the way you want to be managed.

- Bring to mind a sense of goodwill and compassion toward what you want to say. Reach out and touch people's heart as you express to connect between their safety and their relationships with what matters the most –people's lives. How?

- Raise your words but not your voice when communicating

- Be honest, direct, and to the point

- Be brave to speak from the heart

- Express yourself and open up honestly

- Encourage the listeners to ask questions and speak their piece

- **"Open Door Policy" The Norm**: Transparent and 'open door policy' allow and encourage staff to communicate, share, talk and to ask questions. **Transparent communication acknowledges people to have the right to question, and that decision-makers have the responsibility to address their concerns**.

    - Be transparent, open and honest about what you want to hear.

    - Communicate without beating around the bush.

    - Be specific and leave no room for doubt.

    - Communicate on a foundation of trust. Why? People will willingly give feedback without worrying about retribution, offense and the fear of ridicule.

    - Be caring, brave and have the confidence to seek clarification if not sure.

    - Seek management assurance that people inputs will be held confidential and that there won't be any negative repercussions.

- **Speak With Passion:** In the end, it comes down to passion. You've got to 'reach and touch' the people, communicate with passion and at times, try it with 'a tinge of compassion.' Otherwise, don't bother.

- **Be passionate and compassionate to experience the emotions of the people wholeheartedly.** How? Use personal stories tied to the topic to help the audience 'connect' with you on an emotional level to learn a bit about you, the communicator.

- Always articulate safety destination, expectations, and performance levels, and transmit a consistent safety message.

- If and when the moment is right, show up with warmth, charisma, radiate an intense emotion, passion, and compassion, and speak from your heart.

Be yourself. Be compelling. Be who you are–your voice, style, and your best self. Speak with passion, but most importantly, speak from the heart. That's SafetyDNA leadership, and it must start with you and me!

CHARACTER
CREDIBILITY
HONESTY
LOYALTY
COMMITMENT
CARING
RELIABILITY
INTEGRITY
HUMILITY
COMPETENCE
CONSISTENCY
CONFIDENCE

TRUST

"Influence the culture of safety by what you do, what you say, what you focus on, how you behave and how you execute based on a foundation of trust."

Insight 7

"Some Things Never Go Out Of Fashion."
Leadership By Trust

Leadership requires no formal title or position; it's a personal choice. It's an opportunity to lead, talk, provide feedback in a caring manner, reward good behaviors and be a catalyst to help people make the most of their opportunities. Leaders should make everyone feel comfortable, safe, hit a pause, and reflect on their organizational safety culture. Are we creating a safe environment? Are we leading by example? Are we being mentors and guides for our teams?

- **Who Can Be Leaders**: Some demonstrate 'natural' leadership personality traits, habits and behaviors. However, this does not mean that everyone else cannot be a leader. What makes a person to be recognized as a leader has more to do with his or her personality traits. Some personality traits noticeable in successful and dynamic leaders are as follows:

    - **L** istens And Rolls Out A Vision–Visionary, forward-thinking, transparent, passionate, caring, compassionate and motivating.

    - **E** mbraces Change And Assumes Challenges–Drives change, promotes emotional bond and champions everyone to get involved.

    - **A** cts As Coach And Mentor–Listens, coaches, trains, provides constructive feedback and mentors continuously.

- **D** emonstrates Trust, Credibility And Integrity–Walks the talk, accepts blame, interacts and holds everyone accountable.

- **E** ngages And Empowers–Interacts, engages, powers up people and shares personal success and failure experiences.

- **R** espect And Responsibility–Earns respect, most importantly, from their followers and demonstrates responsibility.

- **S** ervanthood–Serves the people and followers to enrich lives, build better organizations and create a just, safe and caring workforce.

Leadership DNA is attainable by anyone who makes it a personal choice and has the passion, care, and drive. Attractiveness and magnetism of leaders, like it or not, is the foundation of human relationships, aspirations and the start of leadership DNA development.

- **Why Leadership Trust: "Leadership is not about titles, positions on organization flowcharts. It is about one life influencing another."[7]** Leaders lead and influence from the front, and build trust based on core values.

  - Trust is complicated to earn but fragile to disintegrate; once broken, it's hard to recover. It takes years to earn, but only a matter of seconds to lose.

  - Trust is the core of leadership traits to foster and promote ownership of the safety core vision and values.

  - Trust is the DNA glue of life to hold all relationships. Why? It's the magnetic force that glues key personality traits together as shown in the bubble below.

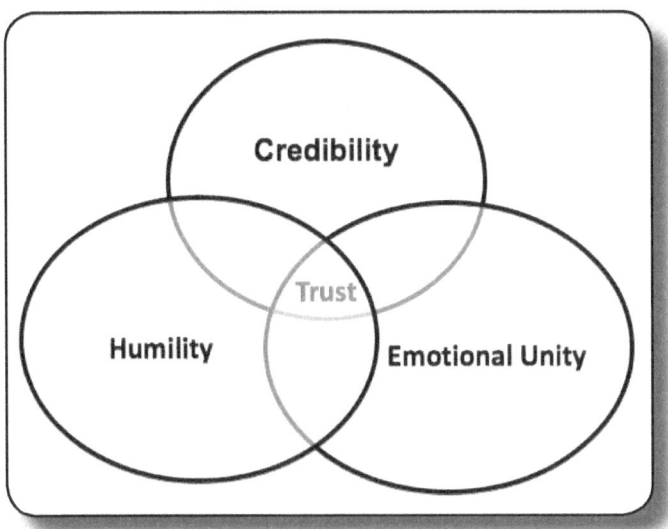

Putting the right leaders in the drivers' seats with the right attitudes, habits, behaviors, those who exhibit safe personal choices, self-discipline and persistence shall influence the difference in our lives. Take, for example, the trust placed by 335 passengers on the aircrew of a Boeing Dreamliner. Even though it's 'a magnificent masterpiece of engineering' built with exceptional safety, engineering, fuel efficiency, cost and advanced technology, every passenger on the plane places their trust on the aircrew in the cockpit to get them home safe.

- **Trusted Leadership 'Wins People's Hearts':** True leaders communicate, listen and respond consistently. They willingly admit and take responsibility for errors or mistakes. So, in life, human beings being human, we do make mistakes as we are not perfect. We stumble, we fail, and times, we get hurt. We then get up, and we try again, but, in this process, never break trust. Why? Forgiving and forgetting is easy, but trusting again is hard.

Life itself does not allow us to go back and fix what we have done wrong, but it does let us learn from our mistakes and at-risks habits to live each day better and safer than our past. It's been said that we come with nothing, we go with nothing, but we can achieve a little remembrance in people's hearts and minds by being human through humility, integrity, emotional unity and credibility built with trust. Give trust to your people as it's just smart management offense and not defense! Why? Giving trust minimizes the risk of micromanagement to avoid doing other people's work instead of managing the team.

Workforce, therefore, tend to seek out and attach to leaders who look out for their best safety. Personal leadership growth interests–win the trust of people. "If someone follows you, then the reason is trust."

- **Credibility:** Act in incredible ways that provide benefits to the people and win trust. A leader's competence alone does not, in totality, result in trustworthiness. Leaders must exhibit a high level of behavioral credibility in what they say.

    - Tell the truth even if it is unpopular or unlikely to be well received. Leaders with credibility challenge the status quo and point and drive people in the right destination. How? Actions are consistent with what they say. They do what they say.

    - Follow every rule and procedure religiously, if leaders want their followers to 'copy and paste.' Why? You can bet that leaders' behaviors, habits, and actions are observed and watched much of the time whether they notice it or not.

- **Emotional Unity**: An emotional form of leadership is rare, but it is required to win the hearts and minds of followers. **"A leader without followers is said to be just a person out for a walk on their own in the park."** If the workforce only hears from management when highlighting nonperformance issues, it creates feelings of distrust, anger, resentment and an unemotional balance. Why? Workforce desire leaders who inspire, who are fair, who are honest, who are trustworthy, who recognize excellent performance and who will stand up for their team.

- **Humility**: Humility molds and blends with trust. It's a thin line between confidence and arrogance.

  - True safety leaders don't think of themselves as superior to any of their team members. Why? They see themselves as servants of the people. **If you view people as working 'under you,' then you tend to think of yourself as superior. If you embrace the attitude of working with or alongside them, you become a people-oriented leader.**

  - A leader's mindset must display humility ("I do not know everything that's happened in the past, what's happening now and around me.") and confidence ("I am willing to learn from you, if you teach and show me how to do it–the expeditious way but most critically how you did it safely."). Why? It brings out the excellence in people, recognizes and values experience and drives winning teams.

  - **Safety Culture Leadership Journey**: **Leadership is a close relationship between those who aspire to lead and those who want to follow, and in this process, don't just create a brigade of followers, but create more leaders.** Mahatma Gandhi said it well–**"A sign of a good leader is not how many followers you have, but how many leaders you create."**[8]

Trust is a powerful, emotional and motivational tool to connect, push to pursue, break and change perceived conceptions, boundaries and walls with people at the different phases of the safety journey. Why? People, being humans, tend to be sighted at various stages of 'comfort zones' in a safety journey. For leadership DNA growth to happen, people need to shed and step out of these zones to get to the leadership zone.

Therefore, leaders create that human connection and attraction through trust to 'drag' the followers along the "Safety Culture Leadership Journey" from authority toward leadership phase as depicted in the graph below.

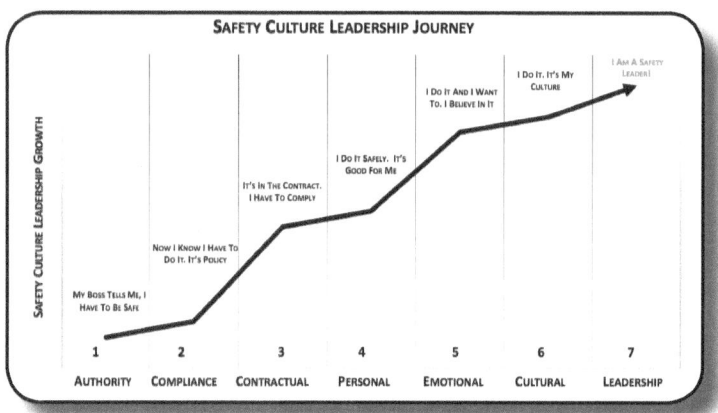

Leaders show courage, challenge to make what's necessary possible and what's essential to create, build teams, promote teamwork, leverage on diversity, connect personal goals to professional goals and leave behind a better, safer and healthier future. It all converges and starts with trust.

"*Leadership is about getting the right, safe, trusting, integrity and ethical behavior from the people.*"

Insight 8

"The Art Of Accomplishing Change And Performance Through People." Be A Leader Not A Boss

The leadership of an organization exists to drive safety and business performances and not to control or stay on top of things. They are there to guide, energize and excite safety performance excellence through people. Leaders establish safety values, develop safety procedures and enforce safety accountability and responsibility for the safety programs. As such, a leader has to be someone who exhibits high *24/7 Safety DNA*, one who motivates and strives to exert a positive influence on his team.

Leadership can be taught. What we see all too often in today's leaders are a little more than egocentric talking heads. They are so enamoured with seeing themselves of camera or listening to themselves talk that they have forgotten that it is their job to solve problems and not create or exacerbate them. It's whether he or she can influence the conduct and performance of others through being an example, motivation, and presence.

Consider the following when working with or leading people:

- **Redefine And Be Forward Thinking:** Leaders must lead by example and be driven by trust, ethics and transparent integrity, and discard old, outdated practices, behaviors, and habits. "Do As I Say; Not As I Do." How? Replace it with, "Do As I Do," to design, nurture and activate a culture *of 24/7 SafetyDNA* leadership.

- **Leadership is a relationship built to think forward–address current and future needs, desires, dreams and aspirations of the people.** How? Take charge, act to make things happen, reflect on the past, share, learn and discover themes that engage and excites everyone else –a future that will be brighter and safer!

- Leaders work for the employees and contractors; they understand and adapt to what they want from the organization.

- Leaders accept and consume failures and mistakes, constructive feedback and criticism as their best teachers and apply them to practice.

- **Successful 24/7 Safety Leaders Prioritize:** As a leader, you likely manage and engage with many people, many issues, different variables, and challenges. Thus, you get pulled to various directions every minute of the day. Having stated this, how to adjust to variables as they change? How to keep focused is critical. It's all about the art of prioritization!

  - **Yourself**–Identify and accept strengths, weakness and personality traits. Why? It enables one to make effective choices to solve life's varied problems thrown at you. It's a universal fact that no one knows everything; no one can do everything. How? **Take care of yourself first above everyone else.** When you know yourself, you understand what motivates you. You resist unsafe choices, bad habits and develop good ones. So, if you don't identify and accept, you can't progress on everything else that needs to be known and done.

  - **Team–Building a team requires knowing that team and not just the team as a whole, but the individuals that comprise the group.** Why? Individuals do vary with experience, skills sets, training, and knowledge. How? Add the skills and knowledge to the inventory to determine how to utilize those specific skills.

After that, divvy up the tasks. Why? To build a foundation of trust to create a work environment in which everyone feels supported–a belief that each member has something to share and offer.

- **Boss**–Everyone in their career has had a boss with a different working style from his or her own resulting in head butts when in disagreements or conflicts. Ultimately, productive collaboration between you and your boss is required to get things done. How? Most often, it would require you to 'manage up' to deliver what he or she needs just as much as it requires your boss to 'manage down' to you.

- **Boss Versus Leader**: Every organization has a 'boss' whether you like it or not. Ironically, there's a massive difference between what makes a boss and what makes a leader. Why? Each act differently—adopt different management styles, build different relationships, make different choices and decisions and being the bigger person!

- **Be A People's Servant**: Leaders give in, respond and serve people's needs, well-being, values, and interests.

  - **"Leaders put their hearts in safety and safety in people's hearts."** How? Leaders have a high care factor. Being a leader is not all about following all the policies and procedures with an iron fist. It is about being human and using empathy.

  - **"Leaders choose to serve people and not themselves."** How? Positive leaders put the interest of their people in the center of their decisions. "True leadership is servitude." Being a leader is not about being in front but about taking care of the team.

  - **Leaders remove obstacles, clear a path free of distractions, streamline processes, find resources and keep the political nonsense out of the workplace.** How? Go figure out and put workforce interests front-and-center to enable work to be comfortable on themselves and the organization.

- Leaders put in long hours of hard work. Why? **With a passion for leading talented and committed people, leaders focus on serving and doing more**.

- **Personal People Engagement:** Frankly, employees want leaders who are passionate listeners and socializers who don't just live in his or her ivory tower or operations offices, but those who visit, mingle and unite with them. Most importantly, they never pass up and opportunity to discuss, converse, dialogue, or debate. They know that their leadership is only as good as their ability to engage, listen, discern, and act.

  - **Leaders take time out to walk and talk to their people at a personal level; take the time to coach, mentor, and train.** Why? Neglect of workforce permits the growth of unsafe habits, stagnation, workforce disengagement and attrition.

  - **Leaders encourage regular personal feedback on performance, practice recognition and praise**. Why? Best and talented people crave candidness!

  - **Leaders pay attention, care and stay in touch on a personal and ground level, understand, influence and expedite their success and career.** Why? Know when to hold off, push or pull to make their people feel valued and recognized.

- **Thinking And Learning On The Feet: Leaders do not plateau off and take a comfort zone upon the assumption of a position or authority in an organization.** How? Continue to excel; ask questions, be curious, never be satisfied, progressively read and learn and keep pace with best practices, technology, and change.

  - **Leaders utilize their skills, knowledge, and abilities, and they recognize that change isn't a threat. Therefore, they adapt to it; sometimes even lead it.** Why? The fastest process to lose credibility with your team is to lose touch with what's happening and show no interest in catching up.

- **Leaders are readers and learners; even after graduating to a manager.** How? Listen, observe, learn, be open and don't be afraid of bad news, new technology, debates, and criticisms.

- **Lead, Practice What You Preach**: Culture of *24/7 SafetyDNA* leadership transformation always starts at the top. Why? If employees perceive indifference to safety among the leadership team, they will adopt the very same attitude. **"A leader sets the standard and is the standard."** Actions must speak louder than words. Some leaders are known to profess and preach to improve, drive and enhance the culture of safety without having not changed much at all. Why? Their bridge between intention and action is poorly defined and seldom crossed or attained.

If leaders talk safety everywhere from formal meetings to water cooler conversations, if they walk their talk and lead the charge, then the workforce will take safety seriously, and actively contribute to improving it. "Quite often, the greatest distance that leaders have to travel is the distance from their mouths to their feet–acting on a verbal commitment." **People see leaders in what they do and what they say as evidence to understand and evaluate the depth of leadership commitment, trust, behavior, knowledge, personal conviction, and action.**

Finally, leaders must create and nurture themselves through their trials, tribulations, and errors. It's not about who is the boss or who's the leader in a moment of time. It's about who gains trust and respect with what ticks in their *24/7 SafetyDNA* genetic code.

To recap leadership:

- It is a personal choice journey, and it starts with you and me.

- It is an attitude from the heart that considers the hearts of others.

- It is not a status to attain, but grows and changes as conditions change.

- It is not reserved for the lucky or the wealthy ones.

- It is not a biological gene.

- It is not a formula or a program.

- It is about people motivating people to get the job done.

- It does not have to do with birth-right, post, title, position, designation or a privilege. It's not born, and it can be taught.

- It is about making others better in your presence, and that impact last even during your absence.

- It is the ability to recognize a problem before it becomes an issue.

"Effective leaders understand the criticality of engaging, interacting and maintaining a good emotional balance while holding people responsible and accountable for optimal, safe and productive results."

Insight 9

"Go And See": Leadership By Walking The Floor And Knowing The Score

Leaders show care with a personal touch and face-to-face visibility to demonstrate that safety is managing and not gimmicking it like it is genuine. "It is not what you expect to see, but what you inspect that makes things go right." **If the management does not own the process, then the process will never work, and if 'management only talks the talk but does not take a walk and walk the talk,' it is a lost leadership cause.** How? It's a process of intimacy, familiarity, empathy and experiencing work life as people experience it.

What I have learned when business owners and managers are questioned on whether they walk the floor, I get some common themes as responses:

1. I don't have the time or energy to go out, walk and meet my staff.

2. I feel uncomfortable to meet and talk, as most workers are not known to me. I have only read their names or seen faces on the organization chart.

3. It's too remote a site to go, and it takes a whole day out of my office.

4. I'm too busy with my job; seeking new business opportunities and sorting out other issues and concerns.

5. My staff shouldn't need my oversight and guidance; they should know what and how to do the job they've been paid to do.

6. It'll just disturb, bother and alienate them if I go out.

7. I'll 'look over their shoulders,' ask questions, or 'hang around them;' all of which I should not be doing.

8. My boss is a stickler for budget and travel expenses; he or she will not approve of my travel.

9. I better not go as they'll think I don't trust or that I'm checking up on them.

10. I hate spending time writing the walkabout feedback report.

So, if you recognize yourself or others in any of the above excuses, then maybe, the time is right for you to start 'walking the floor.'

- **Why Walk The Floor And Know The Score**: Leaders in any organization need to apply a 'trust but verify' mentality. Another way of saying this is that 'people will respect what you come out and inspect.' A helicopter view of your operations site is bad or distant management. All you see is the 'forest.' If you want to audit whether or not the operating site or plant is safe, get out and take a walk. In short, 'trust but verify' what's visible.

    - **Visible management leadership is an effective driver for successful and sustained safety culture management.** Why? Direct interfaces and discussions have proved to be an active process to communicate and drive commitment and leadership toward safety.

- **"Walking In People's Shoes"**: Be a leader by walking the floor versus emailing or texting from ivory towers. Why? Nowadays, a high percentage of managers tend to hide behind emails, SMS and WhatsApp messages to get an issue resolved. Even with constant communication and without putting yourself on the ground in their shoes once in a while, you risk being 'out of touch.'

- People feel invested in a personal relationship with you and in the company as it allows leaders to interact visually. **"If you wait for people to come to you, you'll only get small problems. You must go and find them. The big problems are where people don't realize they have one in the first place."[9]**

- **Checking The Pulse:** Taking the pulse of your organization gives one a tight grasp of what is it that your employees do on a daily basis. A walkabout gives you a real-time pulse of your organization's safety, operations, and people issues. How? 'Stopping or dropping' to talk with people face-to-face gives a sense of how things are progressing on the ground—an opportunity to listen to whatever may be on people minds.

  - **Make observations, collect qualitative and quantitative information, listen to suggestions and complaints of the people and the organization.** How? Use the opportunity to reinforce how people contribute to safety and the fulfillment of the company's mission—show them that their work matters and is appreciated.

- **Workers And People Engagement:** Managers who never leave executive offices send a negative message to their staff. **Executives who only show up at some pre-arranged town hall meetings, quarterly milestones safety or operations celebrations, do more harm than good for people engagement.** How? They project a view to the workforce that senior job titles justify occasional management field presence, and absence confirms that they are away from the business' front line.

  - **"People show care for your operations when people know you care about them,"** is a phrase you hopefully have heard. Why? When managers encounter with workers on their turf, it sends a message that people are important.

- **Involve Everyone, Spend Floor Time:** People resist change without face-to-face interfaces or engagements. It's critical you depend on your people, empower social safety leadership interactions and spend 50–60% of your time with them–'walk the floor, shake their hands,' have regular 'corridor two-way conversations' about safety, smile, keep your ears open and listen-out. Have frequent conversations and pay close attention to what they say and what they don't say, what they love and hate about their jobs, and what they think that the organization should be doing differently.

  - Do the necessary –be an inspirational Safety Leader and surprise your people in an unexpected caring way. People's face-to-face interactions matter. Their thoughts and inputs count. Why? It develops a high morale team to get the best out of them.

- **Ground And Personal Level:** Most of what executives demonstrate is 'all work and no play,' so use face-to-face dialogue to reveal a bit more about yourself.

  - It's a chance to let down your guard and allow staff to voice their opinions and concerns directly to someone who can do something about it. Why? A manager who does not walk the floor can seem distant, unapproachable and even intimidating. Such styles build a wall around themselves and their team. How? The team won't gain from your knowledge, and you won't learn from their experiences.

- **"Dropping In Policy":** Get up from your desk, walk over, talk to people, work with people, ask questions and stay abreast of work, interests, and ideas. Dropping in brings participation, spontaneity, and informality to the idea of open-door policy management. How? It takes managers into their teams' workplaces to engage with the people, listen to ideas, collect information and help resolve problems. People talk virtually on any topic if and when it leads to high morale. Interacting on the ground proves that executives don't just live in their office, but actually can mingle with people.

Go out to the field with a set of minimum expectations to be observed such as:

- Do workers have a thorough understating of work-related activities?

- Do workers understand safety and security-related obligations to themselves and fellow workers?

- Is everyone trained, skilled and knowledgeable about executing tasks safely?

- Are work aids, controls, and procedures in place and in use?

- Have the appropriate hazards and controls been identified, discussed, documented, published and tracked for closure?

- Is general housekeeping maintained?

- Is safe access and egress identified and maintained?

- Are alternative evacuation routes available and marked for emergencies?

- Are people wearing correct and proper PPEs?

- Are walkways free of obstruction?

- Have safety and operations walkabout findings or recommendations been closed-out?

Discussions and physical walkabouts are valuable with executives. Why? As there could be differences between what the executives believe is happening versus what is happening. How? Regular visits give you an 'ear to the ground' and help pick up issues that may not come through formal channels. It's an opportunity to share and invite good and bad news, ideas to improve things, discuss changes, new planned developments and recognize positive behaviors or results. Dropping in for an informal chat gets the greatest returns when you notice what is going on, especially, when people least expect you.

- **"Be A Leader Not A Police":** It's important to use visits to project the image of a mentor or 'coach' rather than an 'inspector, auditor or police.' Meet people in-person to show people who you are and what you can do to help them achieve their goals. Why? Employees prefer to talk in person than on a call or text you by cellphone. So, being there on the floor establishes a line of communication to catch concerns before they become severe and create an incident. How?

  - Schedule regular work time to walk the job sites and the corporate offices so that you get an ongoing picture. Why? Occasional walk-through may, at times, give you a distorted view. Regular walkarounds help to gauge or balance the actual and avoid making rash judgments based on ad-hoc anomalies or hearsays.

  - **Do remember that when you're walking around, you aren't looking for trouble–you're just watching, observing and sharing objectively.** If people receive only corrective feedback when you come around, they'll dread seeing you, and you'll miss out on a significant benefit of being present. How? Look for examples of positive behaviors, habits and safe choices, and speak to it. Ask questions and listen to what people struggle with; know 'what keeps them awake at nights.' Moreover, be aware that being on the floor doesn't mean your 'chain of command' goes out of the window.

  - If you notice issues, talk with the appropriate site or operations manager. Why? You're not there to undermine site authority but to help manage issues better. How? Use the site visit as an opportunity to get closer to the frontline, and be in touch with what's happening to make critical decisions.

- Attempt to walk around by yourself while you're talking with workers, asking for their input. Why? You don't want to put people in an awkward position in front of their site supervisor or manager, and you may find that, at times, you'll get in-depth and honest feedback if you're alone with them.

- **Leave Something Behind:** Finally, leave something behind by way of a summary of observations from the visit. Why? Establish a face-to-face avenue to 'agree to disagree' on both positive observations, moral of workforces and areas for improvements before departing the visited site. How? It doesn't have to be a formal written report or anything fancy. In fact, close every visit out with the debrief conversation over lunch or tea with the person-in-charge and others, if possible. Follow-up with a short email the following day thanking them for the time spent, and say, "Here are my observations."

Running a safe and successful company is a big job. **Crucial strategic planning and work go on in the ivory tower, but nothing can take the place of seeing for yourself what goes on at the floor at worksite sites.** It is an essential part of management leadership quest for safety leadership culture excellence.

'Walking the floor and knowing the score' is crucial. It is a safety leading rather than lagging indicator to allow both workers and management to see and hear you so that two-way trusting relationships are built. After all, you have potentially much to gain as a leader and as a business. It's a great way to keep the company's safety vision and values alive. It's easy, practical, economical and a whole lot of enriching learning and fun!

"Safety Champions are the beating hearts of strong, robust and deeply cultured safety organizations."

Insight 10

"Safety Champion Leaves, Safety Atmosphere Fails."

Changes or transitions in top executive management, or Safety Champions at critical operations start-up and shutdown periods, can or do prove to be stumbling blocks for the successful development or movement of safety leadership culture. Why?

1. **If a 'safety champion' leaves, a void or vacuum is created to 'take up the challenge' or stewardship to implement the safety processes and best practices.** How? Significant top-down leadership impetus or momentum is lost, disintegrated or distracted.

2. If you want to maintain a sustained *24/7 SafetyDNA* leadership culture, you must have motivated 'champions' to reinforce and ensure safety processes and initiatives to stay on course.

Granted, in any organization people do change, career progressions and staff in-out transitions are a way of life; but, such transformations or departures should not happen at the expense of unplanned Safety Champions change-outs.

- **Who Are Safety Champions**: 'Champions are not born; champions are made.' They are individuals who display the following characters, safe behaviors, and attributes:

1. Natural people motivators who treat everyone's safety 24/7 with grave concern and respect irrespective of position or title.

2. Individuals who anticipate and recognize that injuries can happen at any time; whether in the midst of a task, on the road, at home or working on a DIY project over the weekend.

3. Ones who look out for the safety of others and adjust their behavior, habits, safe actions and words to inspire a change.

4. Demonstrate concern for their own and others' well-being.

5. Build an understanding that safety applies to everyone with the mindset that those in charge are not above anyone else.

6. Create an operating vision, show the way, set and hold priorities, keep accountability and lead by example.

- **Safety Culture Champions**: *24/7 SafetyDNA* champions are passionate about safety, and take an active role in safety committees and initiatives. How? Build, promote and energize an organization culture that safety is a core value applicable to everyone, including those in executive suites.

Consider the following to build or assemble a team of Safety Champions:

1. Corporate executives recruit or selectively pick people who display energy and enthusiasm for workplace safety.

2. Keep the right balance of employees, contractors and management representatives in any safety and health committees.

3. Plan upfront, schedule and if and when required, change-out safety champion membership and participation periodically to bring in fresh ideas and best safety practices to avoid disruptive change-outs or replacements.

- **24/7 Safety Pioneers:** For a corporation's safety performance to mature into a world-class safety system, it most certainly requires Safety Champions to drive the following:

  - **Caring About People: Understand that people whom you work with don't care how much you know until they know how much you care.** Paul O'Neil, former CEO of Alcoa said it well with his Safety Policy: Executive Commitment; **"I care about safety because I think it is a direct, tangible way to connect with human beings on a non-debatable goal that is truly important to every human being. Human beings are at the core of my definition of values."**[10]

  - **Establish Achievable Goals:** Establish achievable safety goals to stop or reduce incidents, and commit to managing unsafe behaviors.

  - **Coaching And Mentoring:** Spend considerable time with people to coach and mentor to draw out the best in them. How? Informal chats, not only with team members but everyone within the organization.

  - **Family And Home:** I believe safety consciousness stems from something much closer to home. Why? It actually starts from within the family unit. If parents demonstrate a lack of safety tolerance in front of our own family, especially their children, then it's no surprise that the children grow up with the same thinking, practices, behaviors, and habits.

  - **"Go-To-Person":** Take time to collaborate, relate and get people to see who they can be. **When you open your arms, people open their ears to work, make effective decisions and become better than what they are.** Why? Leadership and decision making are intertwined; for qualities and attributes to become visible, connect with employees, and share ideas and suggestions.

- **Safety Department And Safety Practitioners:** The traditional 'policing' role of the Safety Officers from the Safety Department be delegated to that of a high-level safety practitioner. Such practitioners are to be authoritative and reachable to senior corporate leadership to:

  1. Offer independent advice to senior management on the development of the organization's safety policies and their short, medium and long-term strategic objectives for creating and maintaining a positive safety culture.

  2. Advise line-managers with the development, implementation of safety integrity, monitoring systems and review of ongoing safety performance.

  3. Conduct independent reviews and audit of the safety, operations integrity and risk management systems performance levels.

  4. Coordinate, implement and steward safety initiatives through site-specific Safety Champions.

- **Safety Contractor Buddy Manager:** Establish an ongoing onsite safety manager or champion in the area of contractor management to oversee process improvement, safety relationship, and partnership between company and major contractor partners.

  - It shall be a shared responsibility and a combined focus. How? Contractor Safety Champions are to facilitate the improvement of the contractor's safety performance. How? Through a one-to-one mentoring-type interface of safety expectations and accountability and by verifying and validating the field effectiveness of the contractor safety processes.

  - Efforts and discussions on SHE performance and expectations be focused on the quality of onsite supervision provided by the contract company. How? Determine and evaluate how contractor management establishes and measures SHE expectations.

- Understand the contractor company's approach to safety, and advise how it can be more effective. How? Identify processes focused on delivering results and eliminating unsafe acts, choices, conditions, and behaviors.

As technology and engineering revolution progresses, so will the prospect of potentially unrecognized and experienced hazards and risks that will uniquely challenge and threaten the safety of each one of us. Therefore, Safety Champions are expected of every individual, whether employees or contractors, ones who do not come with an 'off-switch' or take "safety breaks" for a sustained safety corporate performance to be realized.

"*Execute the right choices, for the right reasons, the right way,*
right time and every time, even when no one is watching. "

Do The Right Thing In The Right Way At The Right Time, Every Time; "Even When No One Is Watching"

'Doing the right thing in the right way at the right time, every time, even when no one is watching' is not a protocol extracted or copied from a safety manual. It shall be a 24/7 behavior and habit in all aspects of human life. There are no regrets in life; just lessons learned. Humans beings are indeed not robots, and being human mistakes and oversights are inherent in our natural state. Even the best of us can make errors in judgments, actions or words. Modifying human behaviors and habits through a culture of *24/7 SafetyDNA* can reduce the likelihood of mistakes, and thereafter progressively lower the frequency rate of safety incidents.

Having said that, changing one's or a company's safety culture is acknowledged as not an easy journey. Why?

1. Firstly, years of ingrained practices, procedures, beliefs, habits, and behaviors make it challenging for this transformation to happen.

2. Secondly, modifying the work habits of people who have been at their same jobs, teams, operations site, competencies, tools, and procedures can deem extremely challenging.

3. Thirdly, for people who have witnessed various risk management, integrity systems changes, management and mandates come and go without any changes, change is difficult.

- **What Does Safety Culture Look Like**: In any company, to understand the culture of safety, one needs to watch, study and understand the 'personality' of the workforce behaviors, habits, processes and how procedures get executed and how people react and interact, both internally and externally, within its organizations. The U.K. Health and Safety Executive define safety culture as, "**The product of the individual and group values, attitudes, competencies, and patterns of behavior that determine the commitment to, and the style and proficiency of, an organization's health and safety programs. A more succinct definition suggested: 'Safety culture is how the organization behaves when no one is watching.'"**[11]

Basically, a culture of safety is observed in an organization through how people in the organization go about making safe choices in the execution of their tasks.

- **Why Next Level 24/7 SafetyDNA Culture:** Safety Culture is seen as the personality DNA of the company. Why? It influences the work environment in which people work within the barriers and risks that exist. Having read various literature on the culture of safety, the best way to describe the culture of safety is 'the way we do things around here **even when no one is watching.' Safety becomes a safe, personal decision when employees and contractors buy into the core values and absorb that safe operation is a natural way and the right way of doing business.** When?

  1. Firstly, when a company adopts safe operations as the 'only way it can do business,' people get involved, feel valued and after that, unconsciously and naturally identify safe behaviors, safe actions, habits, practices and work environments.

2. Secondly, if or when it becomes the collective SafetyDNA attitude, habit and approach to safety in a workplace, it determines the levels of commitment in the people to manage safety and mitigate injury risk.

3. Thirdly, it's evident that safety is wrapped, designed, nurtured and activated within its employees' and contractors' DNA.

Here are four values to elaborate on the subject of 'even when no one is watching':

- **Integrity**: Culture of integrity cannot be produced, purchased or contracted. It takes patience and time for such DNA to nurture and activate. Workers with integrity are accepted and respected for their actions and intents.

   How:

   - Workers who have the operative skills, technical skills, knowledge, and know-how of what a good and safe job should look like.

   - Workers who aspire to identify potential hazards and risk exposures unconsciously, and 'do the right thing even when no one is watching.'

   - Workers, no matter how educated, talented, rich or cool they believe they are, how they conduct themselves, treat and care for people their DNA integrity tells all—integrity is everything; a choice between what's convenient and what's right.

   - Workers who do the right thing, when they don't have to when no one else is looking or watching, or when they never know what they have done, when there will be no reward, congratulation or recognition for having done so.

Let's consider what happens when your actions are 'not being watched or supervised.' Ask yourself how you would react in these scenarios:

1. You are given a critical, must execute task which requires working at the height of over 30 ft without harness and fall protection, requiring hand tools but not tied-off and you are going to be working alone. What would you do?

2. Say you have just dried your hands after using a public restroom; you toss the paper towel into the rubbish bin; it misses the trash bin, hits the wet, dirty and messy floor. What would you do?

3. You have a critical must do grinding task to complete with a machine which does not have protective safety guards, no eye protection and it's the only working unit in the workshop. What would you do?

4. After offloading grocery into your car from the grocery cart in a car park bay, you notice the cart bay station to store away carts is at a distance, and you are in a rush. What would you do?

5. You arrive at a non-busy and common traffic light road junction you use daily. You are in a rush to get to work, and you do not see any traffic police in the rear-view mirror of the car. What would you do?

- **Character:** A character of a person displays qualities that differentiate them from other people. Winston Churchill noted, **"Character is what we do when no one is watching."**[12] A culture of safety does shape the character in ways workers perceive and embrace the organization's core values. Talent itself is a gift, but character is a true choice which drives how employees think, approach and execute work when no one is watching. While talent, at times, takes us to a high position in careers, behaviors and habits maintain a high position in the hearts of the people forever.

In leadership, character is more critical than even strategy. Character–not wealth, power or position–is of supreme worth. Everyone's behavior in a boat should be to keep it afloat, row and keep everyone safe, and not drill holes when no one is looking or watching. When people do not respond the way people expect them to respond, then their true character is revealed. Therefore, be constantly watchful of your behaviors and habits. Why? As these can transform into your character and become your destiny. 24/7 SafetyDNA **drives one's character, personality, values, and beliefs of the way things are done even when no one is watching.**

- **Quality**: Sometimes we forget the old saying, "There's never enough time to do it right the first time, but there's always time to do it over again." Always do the right stuff for the right reason in the right way the first time. Henry Ford also said, **"Quality is doing it right when no one is watching."**[13] How? It can be achieved only by being personally responsible and accountable. Therefore, quality should not be just a box to be ticked or workers' lip service only when supervised and watched over. Why? Quality work execution without being watched is the fundamental measure for an organization's survival and growth.

- **Culture**: Some say 'culture is what people do when no one is looking,' as it happens unconsciously in a human state of behavior. How? Through prolonged positive leadership culture, people will eventually change their behaviors and habits toward safety as a core value. How? Organization's safety culture is demonstrated as to what goes on inside an organization by how safely people get their work executed. As such, culture is evidenced in "the way things get done, even when no one is watching"; practices, leadership styles, beliefs, and communications, things we can observe and witness.

- **"Tip Of The Iceberg"**: As depicted in Rick C. Torben's well-known iceberg schematic below. It shows visible, invisible and unconscious traits on how an organization functions and operates–**"the way the organization got things done versus the way the organization gets things done."**[14]

The organization culture, in this schematic, is compared to an iceberg with only 10% of its ice mass visible above water. Behaviors and habits are visible portions of culture and observable characteristics and practices that we can 'see' with our naked eyes. Whereas, a critical part of understanding the complete culture of an organization is the part you can't see. Other 90% ice mass beneath the water is 'invisible and unconscious' which consists of the unspoken norms, practices, perceptions, appetite to change, aspirations, ethics, rules or beliefs, or should I say, the components of the SafetyDNA that guides, activates and drives behavior, personality, and habit. It is that 90 percent, known only to 'insiders' of an organization, that 'unwritten DNA genetic code of behavior and habit,' is what cues, nurtures, activates and drives us as to how to answer questions like:

- Do we have the right safety procedures to execute these tasks?

- Are we adequately trained staff or have the required skills and experience to manage this process?

- Is it alright to remind or insist someone wear a hard hat, or would that result in us being told to 'mind your own business'?

- Should I intervene and stop that unsafe act or choice to remedy the hazardous condition before work, or ignore and go about my work?

- Should we rush to meet this deadline by taking shortcuts?

- Should we STOP WORK, step back, comply with procedures and take necessary safety precautions?

The majority of leaders do not pay attention to what's below the surface. Why? **Leaders generally focus on 'the way we say we got things done,' and not on 'the way we get things done.'** Ignoring what's below the surface, therefore, undermines organizational culture change. Why? Behavior and habit changes, without an underlying process to design, nurture and activate a culture of SafetyDNA that will not last or sustain.

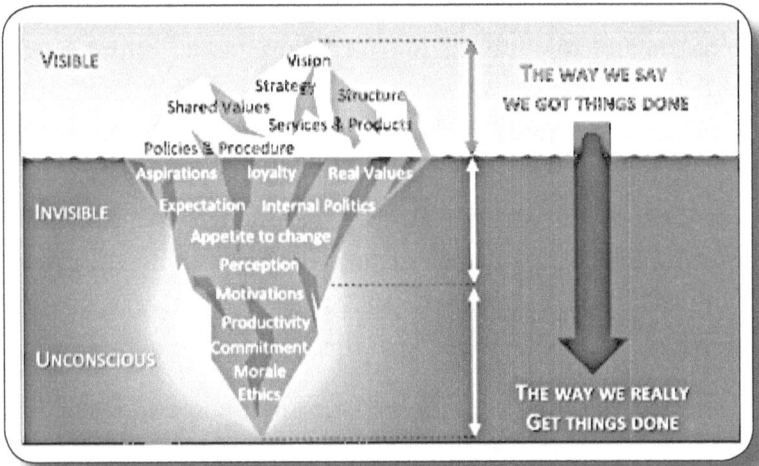

- **"People Are Watching You":** Whether you see it, know it, like it, approve it, or not, people are watching you and paying attention to both your safe and unsafe actions either from a distance, close face-to-face or via CCTV. Therefore, be an example for those working or living with and around us. Because someone is always watching you.

  - Always take notice and be cognizant that 'the way you act or conduct yourself today, influences how you'll act and conduct yourself tomorrow, and in the future; more importantly to your followers.' How? **Your leadership personalities, traits, and safe actions do influence and make a lasting impression on other people–whether it is positive or negative.**

  - **When leaders stop, think, spread, and share kindness, care, love, and compassion, it induces the same behaviors and actions in the person you're helping or while engaging others.** Take note of this as here's the real magic–it does the same for anyone else who 'happens' to be watching! How? It makes a lasting impact and impression on how the observer will act–choose to lead or not lead, begin to appreciate and absorb that leadership practice and style.

- **Leading Role Model:** Our real purpose here in this world–to be leaders and role models for our followers and future generations. To be an example of what's possible, however, small those safe choices and actions might be. How? Everyone is, in some fashion, a teacher, mentor or coach. Some people seek from them; some observe subconsciously due to attraction; some learn by seeing without being completely unaware that they are learning from others by watching. In the end, what really matters is what team we built–what we shared with them through our character.

I am a believer that living your legend isn't just about enjoying your work, taking a paycheck and making a career. It's about what you leave behind for others safety, career development, and well-being when you retire, leave and go away. The ripples of such leadership role model practices and styles travel a lot farther, deeper and are more profound than we think, which, over time, creates a culture of safety leadership.

Every organization's deep safety culture should produce concepts of what is considered dangerous, risky or safe, and what are attitudes, habits, unsafe actions and behaviors to mitigate risks and hazards. *24/7 SafetyDNA* **is indeed, a culture process. It begins with you and me, and it is designing, nurturing, activating and leading it 24/7.** That's what we call *24/7 SafetyDNA* lifestyle driven leadership which must happen 'even when no one is watching'!

"If we approached our lives with common sense from our head to our heart with a commitment that we are all in this together, and that we look out for each other, then there is nothing we can't do safely."

I'm With You. We Are All In This Together. "See Something Wrong, Say Something, Do Something"

When a culture of safety is ingrained in an organization, it is based on shared assumptions, beliefs, and core values. That said, would you feel comfortable calling out your CEO for not wearing safety glass, safety shoe or a hard hat? If yes, it is likely that you work for a corporation where it's an expected reaction. If so, that's great news–keep it that way! On the contrary, many, till this day, struggle to have the courage or are empowered to approach a senior leader, or for that matter, even a subordinate, a peer, and speak up on unsafe behaviors, choices or acts.

Empowering workers to approach, intervene and speak up is a crucial characteristic of whether organizations have deep-rooted, active and matured safety culture. **"See something and saying nothing is like saying I don't care."** It starts with you; that it is okay to approach, intervene or STOP WORK. Analysis of safety lagging indicators shows that numerous incidents and injuries could have been prevented or mitigated if or when someone had shown the courage or concern to approach and have that safety conversation. Experience tells me that incidents do not just sneak up on everyone in the workplace. Leadership simply needs to nurture and activate the habit of the workforce to engage the eyes, hearts, and minds of the workforce.

Here are a couple of leadership tools, processes, and tactics to use:

- **Approaching Others**:

  - It's a mindset process to get people involved with the culture of "see something, say something, do something" for the safety of the people around you. It's extensively used in ExxonMobil operations worksites to enourage workers safety involvement and interfaces

  - It empowers people to interact, prevent and mitigate safety and health-related incidents no matter what roles, titles, and positions they are in an organization.

  - It's an expectation and a habit that we all pitch in, we look out for each other, we're a team, and we're in all in this together.

  - **It is better to approach someone to reduce exposure than to regret not doing so.** Why? The more we approach, 'Nobody Gets Hurt.'

The willingness to take the time to engage our eyes, hearts, and minds, and then approach others is a powerful indicator of the culture of safety and the company's *24/7 SafetyDNA*. Why?

1. It holds everyone accountable and responsible for safety.

2. It promotes the use of knowledge, skill, and experience to help others.

3. It shows sincerity and human care about others' safety and well-being.

4. It prevents mistakes and mitigates hurts and injuries to people.

5. It helps a simple reporting-out process for analysis.

6. It drives people to focus on tasks to be executed safely.

7. It generates a momentum of behavior, safe choice or habit change, as co-workers tend to revert, respond and reciprocate to approach other workers.

- **Approaching Others, Human Behavioral Change**: If you have workers who do not accept feedback in a positive way that can promote safety culture behavior, try the following 5-steps as outlined by the Ministry of Business, Innovation, and Employment, in an article described as '5–Steps.'[15]

  - **Step 1. Approach Your Worker with A Friendly And Problem-Solving Attitude**

    A significant reason why a worker has unsafe habits is because they're not aware they're unsafe in the first place. Indeed, risky behavior is often an ingrained habit. Start these conversations without blame and don't assume a worker is deliberately unsafe.

  - **Step 2. Describe Their Behavior Objectively And Say Why You're Concerned**

    Be clear and avoid a criticizing tone. For example, don't say, "I can't believe you climbed the ladder that way! Don't you know what could happen?" Instead, say something like, "I saw the way you climbed that ladder, and I'm concerned you could get hurt." By explaining it this way, you're letting the person know you're personally worried about their welfare.

  - **Step 3. Tell Them What Action Is Expected And What The Benefits Are**

    Give clear instructions about the right behavior and explain the rationale for this. For example, say: "I'd prefer that you get someone to hold the ladder for you. We want you to go home safely. If that means taking time to get help, I'd rather you do that than rushing and risk getting hurt."

- **Step 4. Check They Understand And Get A Commitment To The New Behavior**

  Studies show that by asking people to commit to changed behavior, they're more likely to change. After your chat, check if they understand what you're asking of them. Then, you could say, "Can I count on you to do this?" or "Do you agree to this?"

- **Step 5. Tell Them You'll Back Them Up If Anyone Questions Their New Behavior, Or If They Identify A Risk On Their Own**

  It's important to lead by example and be consistent with Health and Safety if you're going to create a new H&S culture. It means saying things like, "If anybody questions why you're doing it this way, I can help explain it to them and let them know I expect all staff, including me, to do it this way."

- **Safety Intervention:** Intervention is another proactive mindset process to involve oneself in an at-risk situation to prevent an injury or incident from occurring.

  - It's a two-way behavioral safety process of 'stopping work and speaking up,' document and report-out about unsafe behaviors, unsafe choices, and habits or conditions that you see and not walking away from it. **Speaking up is a key to design, nurture and activate a caring safety culture. "If you care, you will intervene and speak up."**

- **STOP WORK Policy:** It's another proactive management process driven by a top-down executive delegated and approved.

  - **Allows one to step back understand what you are doing, and if you don't understand, you have no authority to proceed**

with work, only influence you to have to step back and STOP WORK.

- Support with a delegated STOP WORK Policy authority from corporate leadership to the workforce that it is mandatory for 100% compliance.

- Promotes a trusted environment among workers to call a time-out, STOP WORK and be recognized; even, in some instances, be rewarded for doing it.

- Prevent injury, identify at-risk behaviors, condition or act to reduce equipment damage and complete task on time and budget.

- **Last Minute Risk Assessment (LMRA):** Another tool commonly used nowadays is to **"Stop, Think And Then Go"** before executing any task as per the simplistic 'traffic light indicator.' It's referred to as Safe Performance Self Assessment (SPSA) in ExxonMobil to be actively used before beginning any activity, tasks or job. It's a self-questioning process just before executing; as a final line of safety defense. Schematics and pointers below help describe the process.

STOP – SEE A RISK!

ASK, WHAT COULD GO WRONG?
ASK, WHAT IS THE WORST THING THAT COULD HAPPEN?
ASK, IF SOMETHING DOES GO WRONG, WHAT SHOULD I DO?
ASK, IS THERE A SAFER WAY OF DOING IT?
ASK, MUST WE DO IT NOW. CAN WE STOP WORK?

THINK – ANALYZE RISK!

ARE YOU & YOUR WORKMATES SAFE?
DO WE HAVE ALL THE NECESSARY TRAINING, SKILLS AND KNOWLEDGE TO DO THIS JOB SAFELY?
DO I HAVE ALL THE PROPER TOOLS, EQUIPMENT AND PERSONAL PROTECTIVE EQUIPMENT?

GO – EXECUTE SAFELY!

ONLY IF TASK IS SAFE!
ONLY IF NECESSARY & REQUIRED CONTROLS IN PLACE!
ONLY IF NECESSARY ACTION TO ENSURE THE JOB IS DONE SAFELY!
ONLY IF/WHEN FOLLOWING APPROVED WRITTEN PROCEDURES!
FINALLY, BE PREPARED. ASK FOR ASSISTANCE, IF AND WHEN NEEDED!

- **Eliminate Unsafe Acts And Unsafe Conditions**: A sharing from **Hebert William Heinrich–1920s**[16] from analyzing about 75,000 incidents is shown against the safety Incident Triangle pyramid. Even though it's based on the premise of human failures, it could also be due to operating systems with which work is executed, or other causes and contributing factors. The key takeaway message for the sharing is as follows:

  - When an organization eliminates unsafe acts, unsafe behaviors, risky choices, and unsafe conditions, it will eventually eliminate ALL near misses, minor injuries, lost time and fatal injuries. How? Start approaching others, implement STOP WORK, perform interventions and LMRAs.

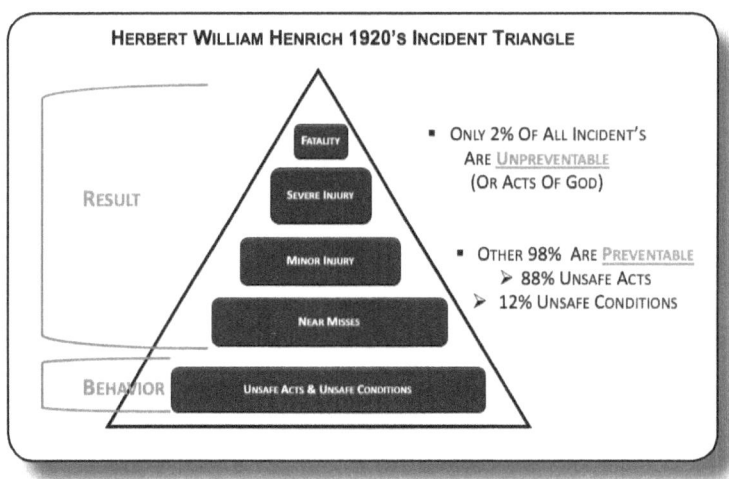

Let's now look at some classic examples of unsafe acts and unsafe conditions that workers might encounter while at their worksite:

Unsafe Acts

- ♣ Operating Equipment Or Machine Without Permission
- ♣ Using the Wrong Tool For A Job

- ♣ Not Using Personal Protective Equipment

- ♣ Using Defective Tools And Safety Devices

- ♣ Horseplay

- ♣ Working With Faulty Equipment & Machinery

- ♣ Incorrect Lifting Techniques

- ♣ Not Wearing Seat Belts While Driving

- ♣ Refueling Cars With Engines Running

- ♣ Using Tools Or Equipment Incorrectly

Unsafe Conditions

- ♣ Lack Of Protective Guards On Machinery

- ♣ Inadequate Lighting At Job-site

- ♣ Poor Housekeeping

- ♣ Faulty Equipment & Machinery

- ♣ Inadequate Fire Fighting & Alarm Systems

- ♣ Crowding Workers Into One Congested Area

- ♣ Wrong Placement/Arrangement Of Furniture

- ♣ Waste Going Into wrong Waste Stream

- ♣ Inadequate Ventilation

- ♣ Unsafe Position Or Posture (Ergonomics)

- ♣ Wearing Loose Clothing While Working On Running Machines

- **Culture Of Caring:** In robust, safety cultured companies, everyone goes beyond 'the call of duty' to identify unsafe conditions, hazards, and acts, and they are motivated to approach and intervene. **Company leaders are the 'catalyst' to design, nurture and activate the culture of commitment to determine behavior and habit change so that people take accountability and responsibility not only for their safety.** If one humanly cares about somebody, one should recognize unsafe actions so that it does not reoccur. Why? Care is of human essence in this world. Caring is a gift that no one can purchase as its roots are in our heart's not just for a while, but for a lifetime as a core value.

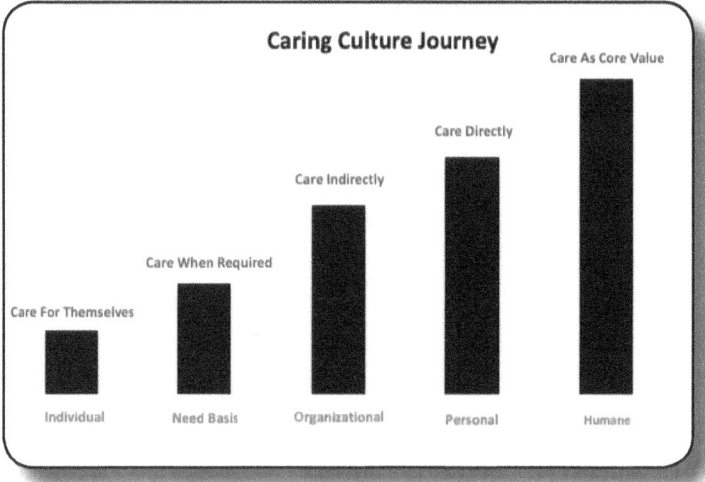

- **Starts With Leadership; Avoiding Criticisms:** Leaders need to be role models. If an activity doesn't look right, begin to ask questions and not give silent consent. It's essential to have the courage to stop at-risk situations and speak up.

  - **If workers don't see leaders intervening, they will not think it is crucial–if it is crucial to the leader, it will be necessary for the workers.**

  - Leaders must stress the friendly, helpful, protective nature of the intervention to correct the unsafe action or condition, without penalty. The theme should be: **"No one should be injured,**

hurt or killed to get a paycheck." Why? Interventions help each other–avoid personal criticism.

- Coach and mentor workers to stop at-risk behaviors, actions, habits or conditions without offending–don't lecture.

- Keep it short. Never ask for names. If discipline is attached to a safety intervention, workers will not intervene.

- **Empower, Question When Things Don't Look Right:** Empower people to stop an unsafe procedure, bad habit or practice as the final barrier to prevent a severe event. How?

  - Advocate expectations with both words and actions

  - Positive recognition for questioning is essential, as is zero tolerance for intimidating behaviors.

  - Anyone and everyone should be empowered and have the authority to STOP WORK when something is wrong or when things 'just don't seem right.'

  - Empower, and not enslave people in a culture of dependence, entitlement, and victim-hood instead of ability and hope.

  - A simple philosophy–"The safer you work, the lesser you get people hurt."

So, what keeps us from stopping unsafe acts or and from questioning or speaking up? Let us review some of the reasoning or excuses:

- May not want to make someone irritated or agitated

- Actions may upset the workers as they may get a sense that his or her performance is being assessed or evaluated

- Workers to be intervened could be friends in the community they live with, or related; so, why break community, family or personal relationships.

- Language or cultural barriers for national or local employees speaking up to expatriate employees.

- May not know where to say it, when to say it, how to say it or what to say.

- Taught and coached to mind their own business and not break working and subordinate, peer or personal relationships.

- Workers have the required working experience and knowledge, done a similar task before and know the risk, but have opted to take the short-cut, unsafe action or risk.

- Workers more experienced, and the observers are younger or less experienced. Therefore, they don't like telling seniors how to perform their tasks.

- Workers desire to get the job finished so can all go home as soon as practical, thus do not want to disrupt or rework their tasks.

- Contractors are reluctant to approach company employees.

Everyone is responsible for speaking up when workers observe a person performing an at-risk act. It's the humane thing to do. Approaching others, intervening and stopping hazardous work is shared leadership responsibility. We're all in this together! Leaders need people, and people need leaders. If you see something wrong, say something and do something.

"An organization's unspoken norms, beliefs, practices, acts and ground rules exist without the conscious knowledge of the people who work for it."

Unspoken Norms, Practices, And Ground Rules: "The Way We Do Things Around Here"

Unspoken Norms, Practices and Ground Rules (UNPGRs) knowingly or unknowingly exist in all workplaces, organizations, corporations, schools, and enterprises, although the people within them do not admit, talk or publish them. **Unspoken norms manifest in peoples' body language such as, "I don't really want to be here," or "I'm here just because I have to be, or I was directed to be here,"** which send a more powerful message than verbal or written communications.

- UNPGRs create an organizational culture and personality that governs what and how employees, workers, and managers go about with their tasks in their organizations.

- UNPGRs perceptions of 'the way we do things around here,' are peculiar. Why? As they are rarely visible. But, their power of influence is a deep-rooted culture; "a way business is executed here."

- UNPGRs can be implicit management's call or understanding. How? Safety initiatives are not promoted aggressively or encouraged as they cost money.

- UNPGRs may get accepted, but received as a challenge or criticism to management's knowledge, skills, organizational practices or authority. How? Senior management could only talk about putting people first, but action at the corporate level shows it is just lip service.

- **Where Are UNPGRs:** Even though UNPRs exist, organizations prefer to ignore, or should I say are 'unaware.' Have you ever been at a workplace and found yourself thinking, 'I wish I'd known about that or this? Why didn't anyone brief me or alert me on these practices beforehand?'

UNPGRs are:

- Practices which exists 'unconsciously' to influence and dictate corporate image and safety performance.

- Unwritten or unstated 'code' referred to as 'hog laws and ground rules' which had originated from assumptions and practices.

- Upheld and shared beliefs passed on by workers, workplace legends and leadership practices, personalities, and styles from employers, managers or company founders.

- Reflections of preferences or standards; the way to conduct operations which have been accurately or inaccurately passed down over the years.

- Differences between what people had said, how people behave, how people react, what people talk and what people do.

In summary, they are part and parcel of a company's organizational operating culture–the unwritten standards, practices, acts, and norms that have shaped mindsets, attitudes and after that, it drives behaviors, habits and actions of the people.

- **Unspoken Strategies:** All workplaces have UNPGRs and navigating your organization's 'implicit codes' is critical for safety, career progression and development growth. While some may seem ridiculous, it's true to say it could unknowingly hinder your progress up the corporate ladder if you're not aware of what is expected of you. For example, even in the age of telecommunications, information technology, and virtual workplaces, long hours in the office is at times 'expected' mode of work culture for career advancement. How? When people see management putting in extra hours, they become inspired to follow the leader.

- **What's Are Ways To Find Out About UNPGRs**:

  1. Observe others and look at what's acceptable behavior and what isn't.

  2. Watch whose career opportunities are advancing, and who's not.

  3. Ask questions about the internal culture, and seek feedback on your responses.

Here are some ways to get energized with UNPGRs:

- **Build Safety Relationships**–Find, seek out and associate with safety mentors, Safety Champions and safety sponsors through informal safety networks or formal safety committees. Why? Having internal and external safety conversations and systems in your workplace or department is essential.

- **Increase Visibility**–Seek safety and projects assignments. Make yourself available and your work visible. Why? So that, accomplishments get attention and high-performance evaluation assessments.

- **Communicate Effectively**–Regularly discuss with your manager what you hope to achieve and ask for feedback on resolved safety issues and progressed projects and assignments. Why? If you want to move ahead, receiving input on what's right and what's wrong is invaluable.

- **Promote Safety Yourself**–Lobby for yourself and your work, and don't be afraid to speak about your work, accomplishments and future goals. Why? Self-promotion, progression, and career development!

- **Build A Career Plan**–Build up your safety, technical, operations and related managerial or administrative skills. Why? They take you where you want to go; understand your strengths and areas you need to improve.

  It may take some effort to learn the unwritten rules in your organization–you will need to do your research, plan, ask questions and observe others and find out how things work in your organization. However, once you crack the implicit code, you'll have better insights into what it takes to build relationships and be successful.

Here are examples of noticeable unwritten rules and practices:

1. Erratic canceling, rescheduling, deferring meetings but focusing work-hours on the business, production operations, budget, and projects priorities.

2. Flexible working is an unwritten rule that says, "It's on the company books, but it's not the way to succeed." Thus, not uniformly used across the organization.

3. Non-stop use of cell phone with SMS or addressing or texting WhatsApp messages while a meeting is in progress.

4. Leaving a meeting repetitively to respond to a routine operations question from overbearing Operations Managers.

5. Overly focused and attentive to lagging incident indicators and statistics versus learning from incidents; with a sense that isn't worth learning or suggesting improvements, as no one will hear me or nothing, will get done.

6. Distracted or not involved in safety discussions, safety talks, safety toolbox meetings–'attendees just there to tick the box to confirm attendance.'

7. Reacting aggressively or negatively when someone reports, highlights safety incidents or significant near hits.

8. Not getting involved or 'switching off' in safety activities and initiatives. If and when involved just working" to show participation."

- **Organizational Culture**: An organization's culture is about shared core values (what is essential) and beliefs (how things work here) that interact with its structure and systems to produce behavioral norms: the way we do things around here. How?

  With UNPGRs, people watch and get noticed, but people don't say what's really on their minds, even if asked directly for thoughts by someone in authority or leadership position. **People are driven by what is most real and meaningful to them, not what they speak.** In these organizations, leadership behavior reflects differing values, which at a time, confuses employees. Therefore, the unwritten rules become the rules to define the culture of that organization.

- **Communications and Reactions**: Another process to be aware and take notice. If people do say or speak up, the following are the likely reactions and responses:

  - "Can we not talk about this subject at all?"

  - "I would not say it that way or offer any thoughts now."

  - "Why not let the boss sort this out and decide for us?"

  - "You best be informed before you invite yourself in to share your big ideas with the head honchos."

  - "Just stay out of this subject and not talk about it."

  - "Be careful; you may get dragged into bigger issues and unknowingly forced to bite off more than you can chew."

- "You can voice your opinion, but no one at the top is going to listen."

Sounds familiar! Such single toxic responses can undermine a positive workplace culture to hamper an individual's collective safety performance and undo weeks and months of team building. **As a leader, it's vital that you not only concentrate attention and focus on what is easily measured, written in a policy manual but the unspoken practices.**

Organizations create UNPGRs where leaders or managers either act in harmony with what they say, or they don't. For example:

- People do watch and steward; if someone implements an initiative but *doesn't* get noticed or recognized by management. If a person goes way beyond to help a colleague, but his or her manager never identifies the extra effort, then one UNPGR might be 'around here, it's not worth your while to help others out.'

- Employees do keep a close eye if managers 'walk the talk' on 'what others say and what they do.' If a manager says, 'we respect and care for our people,' and soon after he treats a person with disrespect, then a UNPGR might be 'around here, managers say one thing and mean another.' It's all about saying something and then acting differently.

- **Management Or Leadership Changes:** When a management or leadership change occurs in an organization, pay attention to unwritten practices and rules that may come detached or attached to it. In some instances, if you change the leader or manager by chance, you may change some of the UNPGRs. If that isn't there, the change will be more difficult. Since UNPGRs had been implanted over the years, even before a leader or manager assumes a position, it is valuable information for any new incoming leader to be aware and to be pre-briefed.

In the current work environment, if you assume that following the written rules alone will help you or your organization to be successful, you are vulnerable to potential landmines. **People will hold you accountable as a leader for knowing the unspoken rules even though they are never openly discussed, written or published.** Use your keen observation and listening skills to learn, understand and harness UNPGRs to lead effectively, and navigate the reality of your company.

"Ask what happened and what aid is required, instead of who is responsible, as there is always a complex operating system and circumstances involved in any incident."

Insight 14

Don't Punish And Incentivize Your Safety Journey. Blame, Shame Paradigm Doesn't Work

Critical to establishing a safety culture in an organization is a non-punitive reporting 'Just Culture' that eliminates unprofessional, overbearing and intimidating pressures, actions and behaviors. For instance, in the wake of an incident, ask who, how many, what care is required for the injured, what resources need to be mobilized and how can we stop this from happening again. It shouldn't dwell on questions of rules, regulations, procedures, violations and consequence management.

- **What Is Just Culture**: It's an organizational culture of trust, learning, and accountability. The following are its characteristics:

    - Human behavioral tool to evaluate incidents, near hits, bad habits or risky behaviors and events to promote a questioning attitude.

    - Workers are not to be punished for actions, omissions or decisions taken commensurate with their experience and training.

    - Gross negligence, willful violations, destructive acts, negligent or deliberate rule breaking, or non-conformance is not tolerated.

- Advocates an approach to an incident robust reporting that emphasizes learning and accountability over blame, shame, and punishment.

- Foundation is based on the recognition that merely forbidding errors alone cannot prevent incidents from occurring.

- Resistant to complacency, committed to safety excellence, one that encourages both personal accountability and corporate self-regulation.

- Creates an open, fair and learning culture by managing behavioral choices.

How can you achieve such a balanced culture? Here are a couple of key pointers:

- **Personal Accountability:** All discipline is issued in a fair, consistent and uniform manner and under normal circumstances where all employees or contractors are given an opportunity to explain their actions before any decisions are taken. How? Draw a clear line between what behaviors and habits are safe and acceptable and what isn't.

- **Fact-Finding Not Fault-Finding:** Employees are treated fairly if the error or incident is assessed to be unintentional or non-repeated violations. However, those who act recklessly or take deliberate, intentional and unjustifiable risks shall still be subjected to disciplinary action. Investigating an incident with a focus on finding fault with someone to blame or shame isn't productive. **Incident investigation should not be perceived to be fault-finding rather than fact-finding.** Why? Fault-finding encourages people to be cautious, evasive and makes it difficult to determine the direct, contributing and root causes of incidents. Culture should be to nurture and activate people to report mistakes, including their own. How? People need to understand that any reporting shall be used as an opportunity to learn, and not to blame or shame and that all shall be taken seriously and acted on timely.

- **'Fear Factor' and Discipline**: Fear and discipline drive under-reporting and stifle involvement. Why? It works against building a culture of safety. **Discipline has a place, but most safety setbacks can be managed without restraint, punishment or consequence management.** Why?

  - When punishment is executed disproportionately, it leads to lower morale, reduced trust, lower productivity, higher attrition, less teamwork, and lack of people engagement.

  - With discipline, it suppresses and stifles reporting incidents, which in turn cripples the organization's ability to learn from mistakes to become proactive.

Working to catch people doing things right and making a big fuss for a job well done is the most powerful motivator. How? While everyone adores incentives, behaviors that discourage employees from reporting safety incidents in any form can negate your safety culture.

- **Blame, Name And Shame Culture:** In such a culture, errors are ignored, not surfaced, shared or sometimes, even hidden. Why? Employees feel fearful, have high-stress levels and lack motivation when decisions are made without employee consultation, detailed verifications and validations of the facts. No one is to be blamed, named or shamed for near hits, unsafe acts, unsafe habits or at-risk behaviors. Instead, systemic causes are pursued and investigated. Why? Often, when people engage in at-risk behaviors or habits that lead to incidents, there are organizational systems, conditions and leadership practices that inadvertently encouraged or created those at-risk practices.

According to Reason (1997), the components of a safety culture shall include: just reporting and learning informed and flexible cultures. Reason describes a Just Culture **as an atmosphere of trust in which people are encouraged (even rewarded) for providing essential safety-related information, but in which they are also clear about where the line is drawn between acceptable and unacceptable behavior.** [17]

How to manage this?

- Uncover, establish accountability and institute positive changes to promote safe behavior and actions. How? If you desire to lead people, do walk behind or with them always.

- Don't encourage or pressure people to resign or step aside if they fail. Instead, hold them accountable and allocate resources to help fix the problem.

- Lead by example. Look after the person working next to you and don't assume their background experience. Working safely isn't a behavior of pointing the finger at people.

- **Fix The Hazards:** Rather than working to create a safe workplace and fixing the hazards, it's been observed that employers would instead blame, name or shame the workers for incidents and injuries. How? Tactics include pitting workers against workers versus taking responsibility to allocate budget, human resources, tools and systems to fix the hazards. **So, avoid categorizing, motivations, or intentions of people's behaviors and habits as these only highlights management prejudices.** Why? Remember your workers are also 'victims' if a serious incident occurs and not just those injured; they need your leadership, care, and support as well. Stop punishing employees without first empowering them to learn from mistakes and understand the potential consequences of their choices.

- **Safety, Quality & Initiatives**: Just Culture emphasizes quality and safety over blame, name, shame, and punishments. How? Promote a process where mistakes or errors do not result in automatic penalties but a method to uncover the root causes of failures. Why? **A fair and just culture improves safety by empowering workers to monitor the workplace proactively and participate in safety initiatives in the work environment.**

Improving safety focuses on managing human behavior, habits such as to lead to rewriting procedures and work permits, enhanced on-the-job safety and tap root cause analysis training, redesigning systems and infrastructure design.

- **Positive Safety Culture:** Incidents, unsafe hazards, and conditions or stopping work for safety concerns, are not to be attached with reprimands, discipline, negativity nor punishments.

  - A significant indicator of a negative safety culture is an organization that reprimands or imposes penalties as the status quo when lapses in safety occur. Safety issue with punitive measures sends a wrong message to the workforce that vibrates negatively through the organization.

  - When a safety system relies on disciplinary measures to its workforce on fear of punishment, consequence management, and ridicule, workers become less willing to be open in their communication.

  - Encourages workers being comfortable coming forward with insights and inputs to the management to understand what circumstances led to the problem, incident, unsafe action or condition and how to avoid it in the future.

- **Continuous Improvement:** When human errors or adverse events occur, it is to be reported promptly, investigations mobilized timely and direct, contributing and root causes results are to be shared openly. How? Effectively pre-plan and develop interview questions for fact-finding for all incidents. Why? It makes those involved in such situations with the blame or shame probability more at ease and willing to open up.

  - Investigate and share the episode at a personal level with the focus on learning and prevention, and exhibit genuine care for the injured person through words and actions.

- Errors and incidents are considered valuable insights and significant learning opportunities. A continuous feedback loop is needed which should take lessons learned and incorporate them into training, educating and process improvement activities.

- **Structured incident reporting programs along the principles of caring for people, environment, assets, reputation are pertinent pillars of highly *24/7 SafetyDNA* cultured organizations.** By their nature, a well-run incident investigation, emergency response, incident management, and reporting structure reinforces attributes of a cultured safety corporation.

A strong *24/7 SafetyDNA* Just Culture is one that allows an organization to balance learning and training with responsibility, accountability, investigates and assesses errors, incidents, and patterns in a uniform manner, and eliminates unprofessional, overbearing and intimidating pressures. Begin by modeling the correct action by yourself. 24/7 Just Safety Culture starts with you and me!

"Close encounters with disasters and incidents, closer than one can ever imagine, luck, as opposed to solid safety management, has been the only thing saving us."

We've Never Had An Incident. "Operations Safe By Massive Margins, So Why Rock The Boat?"

How best can I describe and share my experiences of nearly 44 years at work about safety? My team and I can plainly say it was 'eventful.' Why?

1. Firstly, on a corporate level, even though I had been fortunate to work for world-class safety performance organizations, we had our share of incidents and 'close encounters.'

2. Secondly, on a personal level, we had witnessed, managed and participated in numerous post incidents and accidents: casevacs, medevacs, asset damages, spill pollutions, incident management, and investigations.

3. Thirdly, on an incident frequency occurrences level, unexpectedly a number of these incidents were 'repeat' category which seemed to recur regardless of what you do to resolve them: slips, trips and falls, falls from heights, hand, head, eye, back and ergonomic injuries.

- **Status Quo Mentality**: When working for world-class safety cultured organizations, a noticeable behavior is that people seem to go through a work life with this mindset.

Here are a couple of expressions from people:

- "I've been working out here for so many years; I am certainly going to retire safely with this company."

- "I haven't been hurt or caused hurt to anybody. I'm and will continue to do just great here."

- "It can't happen to me while at work. I am much safer at my worksite versus even my own home."

- "I have been provided with the best personal protective equipment and safety training; so, why worry?"

- "I can't make a difference to the current level of safety performance here as the current work site, and working conditions are safe by massive margins. So, why rock the boat?"

A key learning to share is don't be like the Captain E.J. Smith of the Titanic who is believed to have said this just before his fateful journey on board the Titanic in April 1912. **"I will say that I cannot imagine any condition which could cause a ship to founder. I cannot conceive of any vital disaster happening to this vessel. Modern shipbuilding has gone beyond that."**[18] These words continue to be echoed by many even to this day–incidents only happen to other people and not to them. How right was he? Captain E. J. Smith found this out at the expense of lost lives soon after.

My sharing: Don't bury your head in the sand like so many others. Don't be like the Captain of the Titanic. Act now! The bigger question is how shall leaders manage or change this type of mindset and instill a culture of safety: "I will never be fully prepared?" The universal culture of safety shall be to have no incidents or accidents, no harm to people and no damage to the environment.

Here are a couple of thoughts for considerations:

- **'Aging Workforce' And Demographics**: It continues to be an uphill battle–indeed a monumental task for corporations when dealing with labor which has demographic challenges as follows:

- **Veteran, 'Aging Workforce'**–Operated tasks 'their way' for decades, those who have been 'lucky' and continue to take risky shortcuts.

- **Behavior and Habit Change**–For people who have worked a certain way forever, to accept and change the mindset that there is such a thing as an incident-free workplace, is hard.

- **Composition Of Labor Force**–Part-time workers and increased women labor force, massive rise in temporary agency contractors together with an inflow of foreign and migrant workers both from within and from neighboring countries.

- **Language Challenges**–Cost-effective modes of working as demanded by modern economies created a dispersed workforce, migrated around the globe; highly mobile, multi-cultural and multi-lingual. How? They would typically be unfamiliar with crew-specific communication methods and phrases, operational sequences, methods, and procedures.

- **New Hires & Short-Service Workers** – Changing the thought process that safety is something that starts when reporting for duty, when they get on the job site or when the shift cycle commences.

- **Complacency**: No matter how complex or hazardous an activity, if we do it repetitively, human nature tends to cause us to let down our guards if successfully and safely executed the task hundreds of times; especially if its repetitive tasks. Overconfidence and complacency are prime concerns. Why? Some people get their ostrich mentality and tend to get their heads into the sand, and they ignore what is happening around them, what's changed and what new hazards are out there.

Complacency is willful neglect on the part of an individual. A sharing is no matter how vigilant you are, as time goes by with no occurrence of any incidents, individuals or organizations can or do become complacent and 'let their guards down.' Even with good progressive safety governance, mechanisms and reporting systems, people can "unconsciously" succumb to complacency.

Leaders must not get into the mode that a lack of incidents means you are 'safe.' September 11th is a prime example. How? Immediately after the attack, people were vigilant, cautious and focused on everything out of the ordinary. Now, everyone is carrying on with his or her business as he or she did before the terror attack.

A sharing of possible ways to remedy complacency:

1. Leadership obsession with continuous safety, awareness, monitoring, stewardship, and improvement.

2. 'Keeping fingers on the pulse' to detect and correct performance deficiencies before an incident.

3. Implement learnings from common symptoms noted in incident reports: ignoring warning signs, overconfidence, assuming the risk would decrease over time, neglecting safety procedures, hiring untrained short-service workers, satisfied with the status quo, accepting lower standards, quality of equipment and machinery performance.

- **Risk Tolerance And Awareness**: Risk tolerance does result in incidents as a consequence of overexertion, poor housekeeping, budget and cost reduction initiatives, pressures, taking shortcuts and unexpected distractions. **It's a known fact that all organizations operate at some level of risk. Outcomes are rarely predetermined, and occurrence failure is often a possibility.** It is the behaviors of individuals within organizations that ultimately determine success or failure. Individuals and organizations do vary in their disposition toward risk. Some are conservative, while others admit it, perhaps, even seek it. The simple flowchart process below depicts how one sees it, understands it and accepts it.

Risk Tolerance Flowchart shown below is used in ExxonMobil as a simplistic tool to assess hazards exposures in the field and operating sites before engaging in tasks.

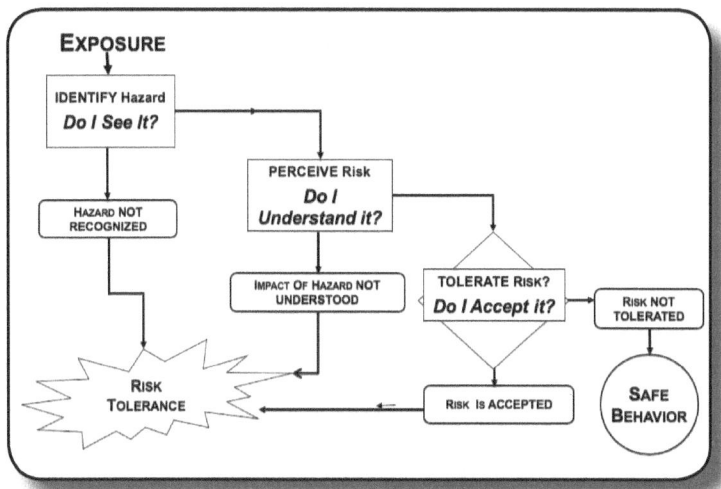

Risk tolerance weighs many factors that influence a decision to either accept or reduce risk. How these factors are perceived, understood and accepted in the mind of the worker or the workgroup affects safe behavior. Rigorous risk assessments of both processes safety (procedures for minimizing risk) and occupational safety (keeping people safe) are pertinent.

Some of the factors that could influence risk tolerance are as follows:

1. Have done the tasks on numerous instances before.

2. Observed leaders taking a similar risk.

3. Did not understand consequence or outcome.

4. Overestimated being in control of the situation.

5. Over-reliance on technology, equipment, and machinery.

6. Cost savings drove pressures, effort, and motivation.

7. Over-dependence on personal protective equipment.

8. Overconfidence due to individual skill and experience.

9. Did not understand the magnitude of the cost impact.

To be safe every day is the hardest job that we ask anyone to do. Why? It requires one to plan jobs such that potential hazards are identified and hazard management and controls are in place.

In some companies' people tend to look for 'things,' situations or someone to blame, name or shame when an incident happens. Why? It's easier than looking for root causes such as: taking shortcuts, overconfidence and tasks commenced with incomplete procedures, poor housekeeping, ignoring safety procedures, a mental distraction from work or at times, failure to pre-plan work.

- **Delegation:** With a 24/7 SafetyDNA **cultured corporation; the norm is for leaders to delegate, exhibit 'trust but verify behaviors.'** Having said that, delegation is a natural and handy management tool for leaders and managers to learn. But, it is the hardest to implement. Why? Leaders could be afraid of an employee or contractor messing up, failing or creating short-term business losses, or understudies to be better than them. What are the desired behaviors and actions:

  Management's Behavior:

  - Involved in everything, and it can be hard to let go. Why? The mindset is that no one can do it as well as the managers. Having said that, managers need to delegate themselves time to complete tasks more appropriate for their level and area of responsibility.

  - Over time, it would eventually get more natural. How? If or when managers hire, train and coach high caliber people, and implement sound processes—watch your team grow without your fingerprint on everything.

  Leader's Behavior:

  - Get things done without looking over their shoulders but double-check the work on an ad-hoc trend.

- Understand that micromanaging your reporting employees isn't good work or safety culture for anyone.

- Encourage a work culture that allows people to work without continually being watched or supervised.

While the journey to achieve zero incidents is far from complete, significant progress is noticeable among companies. Having accomplished that, a progressive behavior and a mindset to further reduce Total Incident Frequency Rate (TRIF) are required. How?

1. Firstly, believe and have faith that mindset change and transformation are possible and required—just because you have been lucky until now doesn't mean your luck won't run out.

2. Secondly, eradicate on-the-job risky thoughts, practices and complacency mindset.

3. Thirdly, try to understand 'why workers do what they do.'

For instance, down-turns in industries (oil crisis) or businesses show that most experienced and skilled staff and consultants are let go by corporate management in favor of junior staff without structured training, mentoring and knowledge transfer or handovers. Even with identified deficiencies, many people and companies seem to rest on their success and laurels; they continue to claim, "we are safe 'by massive margins,' so why rock the boat?"

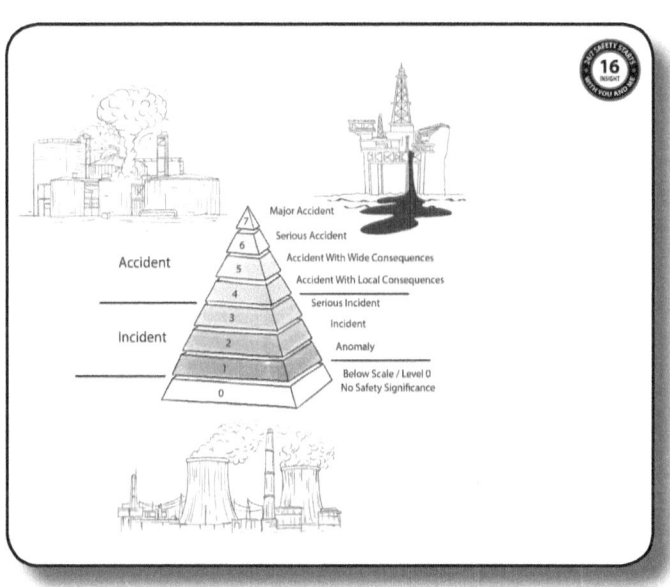

"*Learn and reflect from the past incidents so that the likelihood of them happening in the future is reduced or not repeated.*"

We Cannot Change The Past, But We Can Strive Today To Ensure That Our History Is Not Our Future

Nature of the injury itself is puzzling. In that, people who engage in 'at risk' behavior, do not necessarily at all times get injured even though their chances increase remarkably. Therefore, it is possible for people to make unsafe acts or choices and work within unsafe conditions for a long time and not have an injury. However, hurts will happen at some point in time when they are least expected. The question is what do safety leaders, and corporate management do if or when an incident happens. Joseph Joubert said, **"We must respect the past, and mistrust the present if we wish to provide the safety of the future."**[19] It's clear that when it comes to safety, what leaders and corporate management say does matter.

Here are some thoughts, processes, and tools for consideration:

- **Incident Investigation:** How leaders approach incident investigation is one example where tweaks in actions can have significant benefits post incidents. It is noted in most instances in incident management that early reactions toward incidents by certain quarters of senior management to be an 'excitement' giving a negative impression. How? It's become an emotional reaction as if safety has 'spun out of control,' creating an atmosphere which is chilly, distrustful and stressful. Why? Such reaction kills workers motivation and morale and promotes attrition. Being calm and collective when everyone else around you is going crazy is an essential attribute.

Also, information and facts learned as a result of an incident is to be communicated expeditiously via an email, safety notices, safety alerts or a safety bulletin. Why? The intent is to build awareness and prevent a similar incident from happening elsewhere. In communicating and sharing, start with a simple question, 'How could this have happened here?' to engage discussion on weaknesses, and to get grassroots' feedback that if we do share and communicate effectively, we can learn best practices, implement it in our operations and operate safely and best-in-class.

- **Incident Injury Triangle**: It is noted that it is not machinery or equipment that account for the majority of safety incidents but human behaviors, habits, unsafe actions and decisions. Having said that, the mental triangular image below emphasizes the potential to sort out observations through scrutiny, visibility, reporting, and analysis at the root before it grows into bigger severities through robust safety management.

  After the worst industrial accident in the U.K. in modern times, the explosion on the Piper Alpha oil rig, Sir Brian Appleton stated, **"Safety is not an intellectual exercise to keep us in work. It is a matter of life and death. It is the sum of our contributions to safety management that determines whether the people we work with live or die."**[20] Such safety management effort is to be a relentless pursuit of hazards, unsafe actions, and conditions in regards to their identification as well as to their remediation.

Getting people hurt is unacceptable. Routine and mundane tasks equal high potential and not a low potential for incidents. Why? It is much more difficult to focus on the daily everyday repetitive tasks where people do not think they will get hurt. However, this is where people are impacted and get hurt.

Incident Escalation Pyramid, as shown below, depicts people impacted and severity levels.

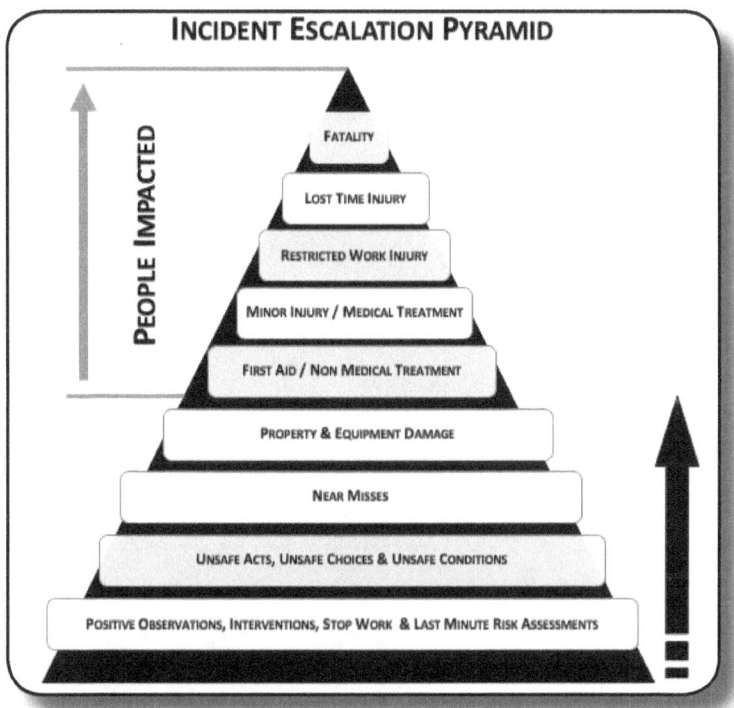

If incident reduction is to happen, it requires an increased implementation and stewardship of simple, practical, easy to implement and use safety programs and tools to manage the bottom of the pyramid where people are not impacted such as:

1. If You Care, Intervene

2. Approaching Others

3. Stop And Think Before You Go

4. Stop Work Policy

5. Step Back 5 Minutes

6. Keep Me Safe-Approach Me

7. You-See-You-Act

8. One Day At A Time

9. Take-2

10. Take-5

11. Positive Work Observations

12. Housekeeping And Hazard Hunts

13. Job Safety Analysis

14. Take Me Home Safe

15. Be Safe

16. Last Minute Risk Assessment

17. My Safety Plan

- **Incident Investigations and Evaluations:** It is essential to identify and evaluate why, and what is responsible for incidents. Why? Some argue that it may be due to careless, untrained and ignorant workers, or perhaps, the 'clumsy, cumbersome overloaded procedures and permits.' We have a duty to report it as it is; accept consequences, learn and prevent it from happening again, possibly at the same site for a different crew. It's called knowledge sharing. Therefore, incident investigation primary objectives should be to:

  1. To identify means to prevent similar incidents from re-occurring. How? Establish events that led to such incidents and what should not have taken place, and compare it to what happened to identify the areas that need changes.

  2. It's not a process to find out who is responsible, to be named, blamed or shamed. How?

- Do not search for a single person, reason, cause or focus on one essential factor. Why? It becomes restrictive, controlled or other factors can go unnoticed.

- Identify the root causes, and determine how these resulted in property damage, injury or fatality.

3. Understand how or why such incidents occur, and how repetitions can be avoided or prevented. Ask:

- Why are these incidents happening?

- What actions are required to ensure it does not happen again?

- What are individual roles and responsibilities to protect ourselves?

- What is this incident trying to teach us?

4. Evaluate workers selection, performance evaluation, hiring processes, training, supervision, operations procedures and equipment in place.

5. Utilize investigation findings and critical learnings to develop and revise policies and procedures.

6. Determine and evaluate if refresher training is necessary to prevent reoccurrence.

Differences in the incident investigation process are as follows:

- **Before:**

1. Unsafe acts and conditions are the two primary categories of incident investigations.

2. Individuals are reluctant to report incidents for fear of name, blame, shame and hassle of investigations.

- **Now:**

  1. Root causes are analyzed for opportunities to improve and fix the system and results are shared widely.

  2. Value of investigations gets recognized and rewarded by the management.

- **Safety Break Points And Near Hits:** It is vital to track safety breakpoints and near hits in addition to the long-term impact of incidents and their costs. Learnings from investigations and careful analysis of near misses or hits based on their potential (no consequences, less significant consequences, or major consequences) as shown below in the Incident Injury Triangle, is critical.

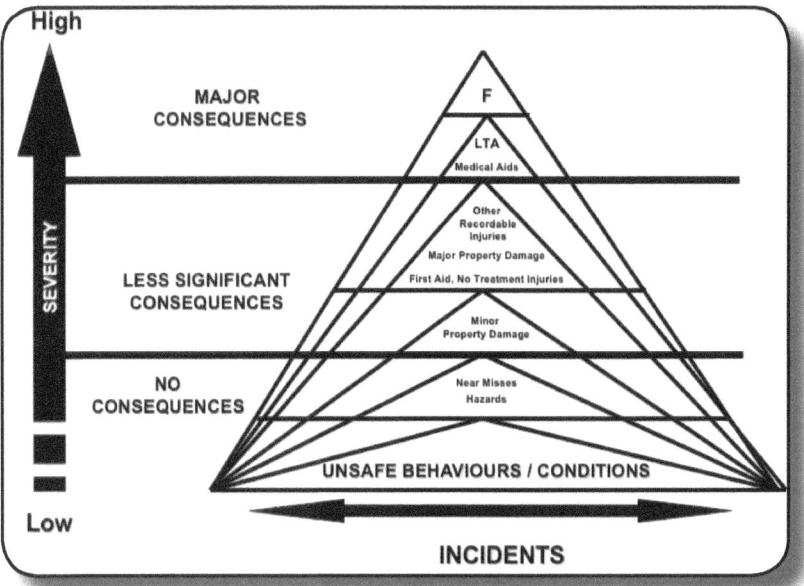

Systems, equipment and facilities infrastructure do break down or fail for many reasons, and as such are not always the cause of the incident. Again, as previously mentioned, further stretching and widening the scope at the base bottom (use of safety programs and tools) segments of the triangle (minor property damage, near misses, unsafe behaviors, acts, and conditions) is critical. Why? It further pulls down the crown of the major and less significant consequences to no consequence's severity levels.

The bottom line is that for people who worry about safety associated with big machinery and high-risk environments, for example, worrying about office ergonomics can seem silly, don't fight this; acknowledge it and work with it. Only proper safety leadership management of health and safety including risk assessments, training, policies, procedures, and practice can one minimize risks to ensure that our history is not our future.

"Irrespective of the company or business, draw a red line between safety performance indicators and business metrics measurements in people's mind."

If You Don't Measure It, You Can't Analyze It; If You Can't Understand It, You Can't Improve It

Leading organizations in safety performance focus on incident measurement, trend analysis, safety, and risk audit results and analysis to explain and understand what that data means and what is it telling them. In other words, such organizations continuously do audit and measure their operations to assess operations integrity, safety system's strengths, weaknesses, and performance gaps to deal with them head-on before harm happens.

- **Safety Performance Measurements:** Measurements should enable leadership to understand why companies are not experiencing the same level of severe or life-altering injuries and fatalities as others. Incidents can and do, happen to anybody and any business at any time, anywhere. Only by good safety management practices, safety incident reduction tools, and leadership management can it reduce incidents becoming to a bare minimum. From where I'm looking, for most, we a long way off.

Let's consider these performance measurement pointers:

- **Why Measure:** Quantitative and qualitative safety measurements are to be evaluated similarly to the quality and productivity of any business or enterprise. Why do this?

1. Identify potential obstacles and trends in incidents.

2. Benchmark safety performance against others.

3. Empower organizations with quantifiable evidence of what is or isn't working.

4. Identify potential at-risk behaviors before they lead to incidents.

5. Set baselines to measure improvements and benchmark against others in similar industries.

6. Provide positive recognition for the company's culture and commitment to safety.

7. Business cases for investment in safety can be justified, and return on investments calculated, or cost-benefit ratios determined.

Dr. Deming had a fundamental philosophy that data measurement and analysis are essential to attain superior performance in every facet of business: How their business is performing, and identifying ways to improve it. He advocated the belief and practice that, **"In God we trust, the rest bring your data."**[21] It's based on the premise that if you do not measure the right performance indicators, or not place the appropriate priority and focus on your data collection and measurement, you are likely to miss out on a set of critical safety performance improvement actions and initiatives.

Remarkably, what we measure in safety is vital. Incident rate, lost time rate, severity rate, and other indicators tend to be inadequate measures of safety. Why? Such indicators do tell us how many people got hurt and how badly. But, they do not tell us how well a company is doing in safety, more so to prevent and mitigate incidents.

- **Performance Measurement Techniques**: Measurement techniques to collect data on safety interventions, evaluate actual observations and results, and implement the appropriate corrective actions which can range from measures unique to a particular organization, use of existing performance measures and standards or benchmarks derived from similar industries. **It should be objective, secure to gauge and collect, reliable and noticeable indicators of performance levels, cost-effective to gather, be owned and understood by the organization.** Also, measurement techniques shall cover the following:

1. Both qualitative and quantitative leading, lagging and personal leadership indicators.

2. Collected, quantified, measured and analyzed with some regularity.

3. Collected data is utilized in business case safety arguments and enhancements.

4. Requires rigorous technical analysis to identify priorities, intensive reporting, statistical analysis on direct, contributing and root cause.

5. Balances its approach between leading and lagging indicators and personal leadership.

- **Key Performance Measurements**: Reference incident rates, it may surprise most, but my observation in safety performance is that it can get better or worse with absolutely no change in safety conditions, behaviors or processes. Organizations can go for long periods of time without an incident despite having an unsafe work environment. How can this happen?–Sheer luck! Organizations which are successful know that there is no place for luck on a job site. Safety is not an accident, and it must be intentionally and purposefully achieved through proactive approaches.

If not balanced, it may fall into these three traps:

- **Luck or Under-Reporting:** Sometimes, good safety statistics can portray an image that everything is 'great and dandy,' and that no one will get hurt. Zero injuries or illnesses may mean that you have been 'lucky.' Zero only has meaning and value if and when there is a proactive Safety and Health Program. In some companies, zero could be due to erroneous or lack of injury reporting, and poor incident investigations. In this scenario, it's easy for the management to put safety focus on the back burner. Why? When the incident rate is low, one assumes all is well with safety. After that, they divert resources and on other priorities such as higher production rates, drill deeper wells, faster tanker turnarounds, and speedier project execution.

- **Incident Severity**: Often injury statistics and metrics such as rates, data, and frequency do not reflect the potential severity of an event, but are merely consequences. For example, if someone is not complying with working at heights safely and falls off from a high platform onto a hard ground for not wearing a harness, it could result in only a sprained leg, an amputation of a leg or an arm, or in some unfortunate cases, even a fatality.

- **Hurt Based Approach:** Traditional treatment-based approach to personnel safety designed for regulatory reporting during the era of legislation is not a safety culture-based approach. Why? It does not focus on caring for people. Whereas, Hurt Based Approach is one that all injuries are preventable by better design engineering, operational practices, maintenance or monitoring. It is based on the principle that all incidents are to be assessed for both actual and potential consequence and learnings to prevent future hurts focused on caring for people first.

- **Safety Performance Indicators:** Safety measurement 'indicators' are required to be identified and monitored regularly to:

  1. Determine the current safety standard in organizations.

  2. Effects of proactive safety work.

  3. Anticipate or project emerging issues.

4. Add value to provide information on the progress and current status of safety strategies, and processes applied to mitigate hazards and risks.

So, if you want to assess safety effectiveness, you'll have to take a holistic, multi-dimensional approach—one that incorporates the three types of safety indicators—lagging, leading and personal leadership.

1. **Leading Indicators:** Proactive, varies widely, predicts trends, and then, drives safety activities to prevent and control future injuries and improvements to the safety systems. It measures the company's safety integrity and risk management system effectiveness and scope or reliability of established barriers that control human exposure to hazards. For example, safety training, employee perception surveys, safety audits, safety inspections, behavior sampling, number of audits performed, percent safe and positive unsafe behaviors observed, stop cards and the frequency of safety committee meetings.

   Leading Indicators Drawback: It reflects what to do to become safer, but it doesn't state the impact of such initiatives. How? It portrays an impression of doing many things, but not achieving anything; thereby, it misleads the perception of company safety performance.

2. **Lagging Indicators:** They are downstream focused on compliance with safety rules and regulations to measure past incidents and injuries. It reflects what and how a lack of safety culture results in injuries, and its financial cost and trends of events including the duration, scope, magnitude or frequency of uncontrolled human exposure to hazards. A Total Recordable Incident Rate (TRIR) is used as an indicator across industries. It does not pay attention to how many employees there are, only the number of recordable injuries and the total amount of hours worked.

Lagging Indicators Drawback: It's reactive; it tells you how many people got hurt and how badly, but not how effective your safety systems are or how well your company is doing at preventing incidents. How? Its injury statistics reflect the outcomes and not causes; the actual condition of the safety climate is not revealed. It's a poor gauge of prevention, as it leads to complacency when, in fact, there might be numerous unsafe conditions, practices and risk factors present in the workplace that can contribute to future injuries. It does not measure what has not happened–risks taken by employees but no accident.

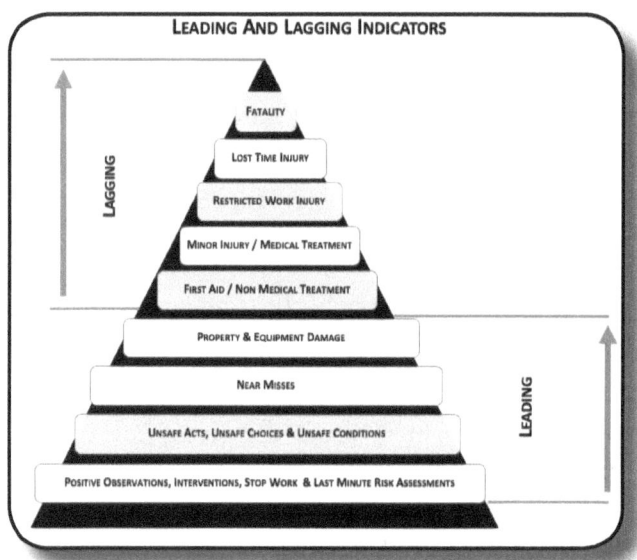

3. **Personnel Leadership Indicators:** Such indicators target all levels of the organization, with metrics related to leadership of the team and individual worker contributions. How? Focuses on critical metrics as significant drivers for improving safety performance. Such an indicator is reported and summarized for corporate leadership review and stewardship to identify potential safety improvement opportunities. Examples below are widely used in ExxonMobil to manage and steward field operations:

1. % Management Field Walkabouts completed versus targeted.

2. % Planned On-The-Job Task Observations completed versus target.

3. % Job Safety Analysis (JSA) Quality Review/Assessments completed versus target.

4. % Integrity Critical Contractor Management Interface Meetings held versus target.

5. % Work Permit Quality Review/Assessments completed versus target.

Overall, my take is that there are no 'one-size-fits-all' performance measurement indicators. Therefore, corporate governance and management need to understand which indicators are usable or applicable to what, when, where, with whom and which industries.

- **Proactive Behaviors**: Safety performance measures should be designed to focus on dynamic, safe proactive behaviors and positive observations that track and report-out what people do every moment. Proactive or 'upstream' positive activities and programs shall be tangible such as numbers of unsafe acts, unsafe observations, active interventions, STOP WORK, the number of inspections, stop cards and safety audits which mostly reside at the bottom of the safety pyramid.

Herbert William Heinrich's[22] take-home message encourages employers to control hazards and not merely focus on worker behaviors and habits, but one that reduces the number of near misses or hits. Why? With the reduced chance of the fatality occurring, it simultaneously lowers the frequency of at-risk behaviors. The only place where organizations have prime control over the outcome of their safety performance is at the bottom of the pyramid.

- **Contractors Safety Measurement**: Measuring safety performance is easier said than done, especially, for companies with large-scale contractor staffing. Why? It isn't a question of just carrying out periodic contractor worksite safety and technical inspections and reviews. Nor is it a question of analyzing workplace incidents as a yardstick.

  With no easy solution for measuring effectiveness, many contractor companies nowadays use tools and processes such as prequalification of contractors, contractor safety performance evaluation and contractor safety training monitoring and compliance. Tech-savvy companies use wearable technology (smart helmets), tablets, smartphones, robotics, sensors, automation, and drones.

- **Reporting Measurements:** It's a process to promote hurt free and to document hurt-free days on daily report and the daily summary of management—recognizing hurt-free milestones and discussing progress at reviews with senior leadership. **Reporting shall be 'about caring for the individuals where we can go in and analyze those injuries and prevent future hurt.'** It's a management scorecard aimed to improve safety conditions and safe practices. How? Daily and weekly accountabilities elevate safety to an equal playing field with other business such as production and help make safety a core value for all.

- **Safety Climate Measurement:** It's a measurement that covers people's perceptions and attitudes of how the organization views the current effectiveness of safety improvement efforts of leadership, co-worker's participation and engagement in work procedures and compliances. Safety climate is recommended to be measured via proven psychometric surveys of various dimensions, either an annual or bi-annual cycle, to provide an indicator of a positive safety culture. Similarly, how the organization does address the findings of such surveys provides an index through which the workforce's *24/7 SafetyDNA* culture can be assessed and measured.

- **Performance Benchmarking**: It's a critical process to help companies determine how they 'stack up' against their competition and peer organizations. Why? It's informative, and it represents the extent to which they are better or worse than industry averages for an apples-to-apples comparison. Benchmarking is more than taking another organization's safety programs and copying them. How? It requires research to identify aspects of safety activities that result in superior performance, and tailor them so similar outcomes can be replicated. Meaningful benchmarks use successful performance results from related industries as a safety culture survey and safety audit programs.

Establishing, collecting, analyzing and measuring safety performance is a challenge, but it is imperative. Failing to measure it, analyze it, understand it and improve it does create expose to enormous risk, undermines your safety program and hurts your bottom line. Doing it boosts not only efficiency, productivity, and competitiveness, but also survivability, continuous improvement and profitability—all good things for both people and companies.

Treat safety both as an art and a science:

- *Art: Dealing with an organizational culture as an art of life.*

- *Science: Dealing with technology and engineering as a part of work life.*

Insight 18

"Look What We Have Accomplished, Nobody Got Hurt Today."

Some debate that if you aim for the impossible, you will never reach your goal. So, with me, I opted to set a challenging best-in-world-class Total Recordable Incident Frequency Rate (TRIFR). The aim is to accomplish a 'nobody gets hurt each day' and strive to sustain previous day's, week's, month's or year's record, and if that achieves a zero, then all is well and great. There again is the awareness that one unfortunate recordable incident in any day would compute to a 100% increase in the recordable safety statistics that would reset the incident-free safety clock!

Do these recordable statistics compute that you are doing bad? Surely not. However, in a statistical TRIFR injury indicator definition, it does indicate so. Having said that, if you don't aspire to achieve zero, then by definition, you have accepted a performance standard which will drive up your incident rate. Therefore, while I do subscribe that a zero will be achieved, it will not be sustained for extended periods. Consequently, I have opted to take it by the day–aim for zero each day.

Let's consider how to manage incident-free days:

- **Why Do Incidents Happen:** Many incidents which I have witnessed, demonstrate that well-intentioned and conscientious people failed to recognize a work hazard, became complacent or took-short cuts. In some cases, even if or when the risk was identified, a decision was made collectively as a team or individually to proceed with the tasks.

Here are some reasons why incidents happen:

1. **Unforeseeable**: Lack of experience, training, and skills, language barriers, no structured risk assessment processes and systems, working with machinery that lack the manufacturer's engineering data or historical integrity performance records.

2. **Random machinery, infrastructure or equipment failure**: Design, infrastructure set-up or assembly, poor quality of materials, operational practices, training, maintenance, and physical construction.

3. **An imperfect person or worker:** A careless moment or someone in the wrong place at the wrong time, lack of training, new hires or short-service workers.

4. **Mishaps, nature or an act of God**: Weather, floods, fires, volcanoes, tsunamis or earthquakes due to the lack of a set pattern, poor weather detection mechanisms, poor upfront planning and lack of emergency response or disaster management funds.

5. **Sabotage or terrorism:** As intentional and strategic upfront planned attacks caused its injuries or hurts. Thus, it's not safety, but I would rather bucket this as security issues.

- **No Injury Is Acceptable:** Absolutely, isn't it? Some of you probably know the injured as a workmate, close friend, neighbor or someone who lives in the same community. Sadly, in some companies, management accepts 'industry average,' 'better than average,' or 'a bit better than last year' as injury frequency acceptable level for their organizations. Such standards of acceptance cause the safety performance incident frequency level to plateau out. What happens in such organizations? Injury frequency rates in such organizations tend to run at a certain, 'acceptable plateaued level' for a while until a series of serious injuries, or in some cases when senior management itself decides that the safety performance level is no longer acceptable. So, what do they do?

- Management makes noise, delivers a couple of choreographed safety speeches, employs a team of safety consultants for safety survey, rolls-out risk assessments or increases refresher safety training. In some instances, management may opt to churn out more procedures and checklists. Such actions get some people's attention and possibly drive injury Incident Frequency Rate down to a 'management acceptable' level.

- After two or three years, or sometimes a lesser period, on the new attained, 'acceptable management plateau' the Incident Frequency Rate starts to creep up again. So, what happens now? Management repeats the same process as mentioned previously. However, this time, they do it a bit louder, harder and with more visibility.

Now, the bigger question is what your company's comfort zone with injury frequency rates is? Is it better than the industry average?

- **"Nobody Gets Hurt On My Watch":** The question on everyone's minds is, 'what's the culture of safety that you want to create?' The answer shall be a *24/7 SafetyDNA* culture that achieves an injury-free workplace by caring for people. It shall be a journey that encourages the leadership to not be discouraged by ad-hoc incidents that hit them and break extended hurt-free records. How?

  - Confront incidents objectively, not as a situation that has 'spiraled out of control' when safety performance is sub-par.

  - Take it one-day-at-a-time.

  - Do not overreact when a setback occurs, as there are going to be many, many, many good days, and once in a while, a 'bad' day at work.

  - **For everyone to enjoy the safety journey, it's difficult for those who compare it, and worst for those who criticize it.**

In the real world, you will have milestones and record-free stretches that are going to get broken; then, the restart button is pressed. Safety records are set by the people, and sadly, other than acts of God, get busted by the people. Don't overreact to those negative setbacks. **Remember, it's a journey. Its direction is more critical than its speed. Being humans, we sometimes get busy looking at our speedometer during our destination and forget the journey.**

- **Are All Accidents And Incidents Preventable?**

  Many have debated that 'some things just cannot be prevented.' Why? It's probably a reason why acts of God are not considered or recorded as 'incidents.' I think it is, at best, a great ideology, vision and a journey well intended to achieve, but hard to sustain.

  If we reduce at-risk odds against us with every improvement to design, engineering, ergonomics, observation monitoring, and reporting, maintenance, operations, training, PPE, operational procedures and so on, collectively, we could raise the probability in our favor. Having said this, let's be mindful that every incident being preventable does not mean it could have been mitigated or avoided by the victim. Why? Sometimes, the event needs to be pre-mitigated with the help of the manufacturers, designers, constructors and most certainly, co-workers working, or the leader of the victim.

  Positively, many people known to me have worked their entire career in companies without a single work-related incident. The day they retired and walked out of the worksite have left behind a deep safety thought, "Look at what I have accomplished. I did not get hurt; you can do it too."

In spite of the resistance and all the debates out there, I believe:

1. Firstly, that all incidents are preventable.

2. Secondly, if you care for your people, it is the only right culture of safety to instill and hybrid in your organization.

3. Thirdly, any other culture invites compromise. Thus, we must set and sell the expectation of 100-percent compliance.

4. Fourthly, keep in mind that the world has and continues to be populated with examples that used to be thought of as undoable and unachievable.

Let's take to heart and get on that 'all incidents are preventable.' We cannot mitigate or prevent everything, but that doesn't take away our responsibility and accountability to focus and be relentless as we can within reasonable boundaries. **No matter how slim the chances are, if there is that chance, then that very incident should be mitigated, reduced or prevented.** If we steadily work systematically and structurally, we can do it!

Steady progress and 'evolution of the *24/7 SafetyDNA* genetic code' is a great way to go and nurture the heart of that excellent culture of safety management.

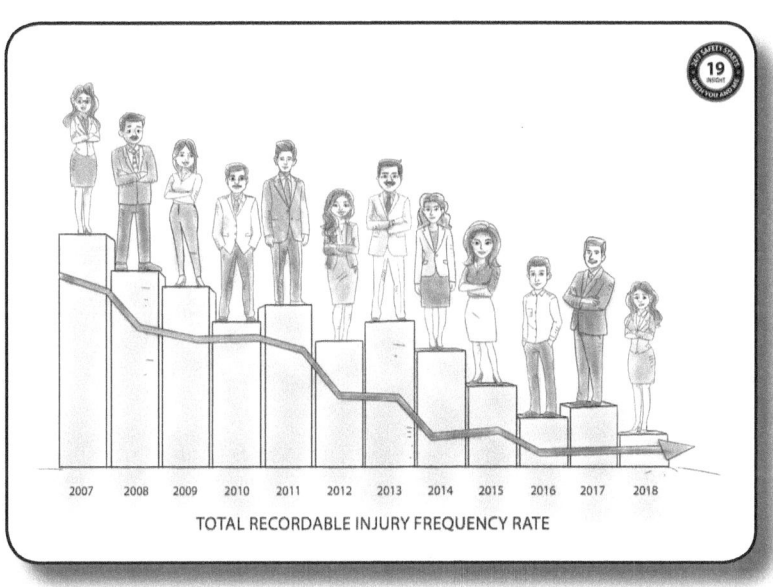

TOTAL RECORDABLE INJURY FREQUENCY RATE

"Safety incentive program is to be designed to transform good safety management into stellar safety management."

Insight 19

Reward The Right Safe Behaviors, Celebrate Success

Whether a company's goal is to improve or maintain an existing safety record or a stellar safety performance, the incentive program is an excellent vehicle. Why? It helps to push the momentum of the right safe choices, behaviors, and habits in the right direction. People work for a paycheck, but they will go an extra mile for recognition, incentives, rewards, benefits, and praise. It is just basic human behavior.

Before any incentive program is introduced, a company must have the following:

- Implemented and established a corporate safety program and have trained and skilled resources (safety organization and committees, accident investigation teams, emergency response and damage control teams, risk assessment tools, safety training resources) to steward the program.

- Accumulated some run time of their Total Recordable Injury Frequency Rate (TRIFR) and operating hours.

Caution! Some companies do misconceive that an incentive program is the 'golden nugget' that will bring results. Therefore, they tend to ignore other safety initiatives. How? Incentive programs can either be rolled-out with excellent positive returns or misconstrued and misused with disastrous negative consequences. In reality, it's not the incentive tool that is at fault, but rather a poor rule design, roll-out, and administration of the incentive program. How? It can unconsciously create peer pressure to hide near hits, hurts, and injuries through lack or inaccurate incident reporting.

- **Incident Versus Rate-Based Incentive Programs**: Implementation shall not sidetrack new managers or leaders, what types of incentives and values to offer. Instead, incentive programs should be intended to lead to meaningful long-term incentives. The crucial question is not what incentives but what behaviors, safe choices and habits need to be cultivated, recognized and rewarded.

With that said, there are two types of incentive programs:

- **Incident Rate-Based:** Rewards such as bonuses, high-valued vouchers, gift as prizes given for no or a low total recordable incident rate of work-related hurts, injuries, and illnesses. Such awards are awarded at the specified frequency (monthly, bi-monthly, quarterly, 6-monthly or yearly). It should be warned that incident rate-based programs in some instances due to peer pressure 'may' tend to discourage accurate incident reporting.

- **Behavior-Based:** Awards for identifying hazardous and unsafe conditions, implementing safety improvements, making safety suggestions, spotting close calls and near hits, achieving behavioral safety goals, perfect safety meetings attendance record, safety committees and incident investigation team members and employees nominated by their peers as having a 'safety first culture.' Behavior-based awards are focused on proactive leading indicators to upfront identify, mitigate or prevent an injury from occurring.

Irrespective of the type of incentive program, it's imperative that management measure both leading (behavior-based) and be lagging (incident-based) programs.

- **Right Ways To Recognize:** It's not the nature, size, type or value of the award or recognition that is of significance. Instead, how the appropriate award was recognized, promoted and encouraged in a meaningful way is significant.

- **Unwavering**–Orderly implementation and administration of incentive policies, guidelines, and procedures to reward and acknowledge the workforce along established and approved incentive program guidelines. Why? Workers must not feel like his or her safe choices, behaviors or participation will go unnoticed and not rewarded by management.

- **Promptly**–Rewards, whether material or verbal acknowledgments are to be given expeditiously. How? They are awarded soon after it has been accomplished to boost the impact on connecting between safe choices, behavior recognition, and the reward.

- **Noteworthy**–Seek inputs from the workforce on what awards will motivate workers. Use a survey to evaluate the type of preferred awards. Why? Incentive programs thrive and mature if based on employees' inputs and participation.

- **Wholeheartedly**–Benefits be conveyed and recognized sincerely so that workers perceive it as an act of their leadership. Why? It improves the working relationship; it is a critical element of a productive safety management program.

- **Management Commitment**–Line management should drive the safety incentive program and not the safety department personnel. How? Corporate governance is to provide the impetus for safety performance through approval of incentive programs and budgets, while actual execution is line management.

Types Of Recognition

- **Leaving Messages With A Token**–Leaving a small handwritten management note with a simple-valued safety token (a safety pin or a safety sticker) at a workstation goes a long way.

- **Giving A Pat On The Back**–A management pat is a compliment that costs nothing. However, it can contribute to a positive forward safety attitude momentum for employees and contractors.

- **Saying Thank You**–A simple management thank you, "Thanks for the suggestion. Thank you for keeping me safe." Or, "Thank you for watching out for me," can be powerful, and are great boosters of self-esteem. How? It doesn't cost a thing, and it can make a huge difference. Two small words that require you nothing, but their meaning is priceless.

- **Tangible, Visible Media**–Recognize and celebrate success via safety newsletters, memos, and other internal communication media. Make posters, print t-shirts, design jackets, print stickers and make hats, caps or badges to identify team members. How? The management has to give them out in visible gatherings like company safety meetings, safety lunches, dinners or safety management forums or engagements.

- **On-The-Spot Token**–An immediate, on-the-spot recognition has an enormous impact. How? Such visible efforts (safety breaking news) among other co-workers shows appreciation for a job done safely, encourages the recipient and others and promotes such positive behavior to be repeated.

- **"Tell-All–Our Safety Stars"**–Sponsor short time-out breaks with refreshments or snacks when safety performance targets are achieved. Use time-outs to seek inputs and feedback on ongoing safety issues, concerns, and challenges. Why? It shows interest and appreciation in what people do to keep themselves and people around them safe – it enhances positive feelings about people's secure job.

- **Safety Slogans**–Popular, visible and readable initiative that does not require specialized knowledge or skill to invent and exhibit. How? It promotes workforce to think about safe work practices and ways to mitigate and prevent incidents. Even if they don't submit an idea, spending a little time and effort to contemplate the importance, mental image recycling and nurturing in their minds about the culture of safety is priceless.

- **Safety Participation Award**–Awards given out to workers who proactively participate in safety initiatives. How? Such awards show recognition for involvement, and again, it encourages the positive, safe behaviors and habits to be repeated.

- **Point-Based System**–Award points based on proactive safety actions and behavior to be redeemed as award items. Points accumulated do not have expiry dates. Participants view printed or on-line award catalogues to select awards of their choice. Safety points allow management to spread around to as many people as possible–those who have actively engaged in the safety and health management programs.

- **Spot Awards**–Simplified approach to identify the desired safe behavior for immediate supervisors to give awards when the workforce do something safety impressive such as:

  1. Approach workers when in unsafe acts or conditions

  2. Identify a hazard or condition and rectify on-the-spot

  3. Immediate reporting of an injury or a hazardous condition

  4. Suggest ways to mitigate or prevent injuries and hurts

  5. STOP WORK if or when in an unsafe act or condition is noticed

  6. Intervene co-worker about hazards and at-risk or hazardous behavior

- **Safety Stars Program**: Worker caught doing it right (behaviors, reporting, participation in safety talks or inspections.) How? Thank the employee for their impact on the safety program. Provide them with a hard hat sticker (shaped like a star) to be placed on their hard hat or workstation.

- **Safety Incentives Alternatives:** Rather than attempt to 'buy-out' commitment, consider 'buy-in' techniques to engage everyone to take personal responsibility for safety as follows:

  - **Make Safety A Core Value**–Make decisions that reflect the philosophy of 'Safety First-Production Will Follow.' How? Start any or all meetings, forums, workshops, seminars with a Safety Moment or a Safety Chat as the first subject on the agenda.

  - **Reward Right Safe Performer**–Institute safety performance as the first dimension of the employee's performance appraisal assessment. Salary and merit increases, specialized training, promotions, and other rewards are contingent on proactive safe attitude and behavior. Safety is to be communicated as a condition of employment, and dismissals for intentional or repeated safety violations. Why? Such a process will instill to alter 24/7 *SafetyDNA* genetic code in workers to take safe behavior seriously.

  - **Employees Safety Involvement**–Participation in safety activities that make their workplace safe including safety committees, site safety inspections, safety walkabouts, incident investigations, safety suggestions, and safety survey programs. How? Time is given to participate during their regular work hours, and efforts are recognized.

  - **Set High Safe Behavior Expectations**–Clearly state safety expectations so that everyone will follow safety procedures and compliance with personal protective equipment. How?

Carefully record, safety performance measurements, publish lost-time incidents and watch the numbers and statistics closely.

- **"Close Call" Alert**–Implement effective, one-pager, pocket-sized and checklist type reporting tools. Why? Encourage employees to easily report-out unsafe conditions that could lead to recordable incidents and injuries into Safety Suggestion Boxes.

- **Creating & Implementing Incentives:** Consider the following:

  - **Corporate Identity**–Develop and rely on low-cost gifts and awards with a high perceived return on value. Gifts that reinforce, display and printed or embossed with corporate identity, colors, logo, and slogan can spark high interest among the workforce. Why? Awards eventually become collector's items of ownership and lifetime display in their homes.

  - **Workforce Culture**–Adapt an incentive program to fit the culture of your workforce and the timing of the award. How? Correlate to demographics of your workforce: age, rate of turnover, spoken language, geographic location, festive seasons and racial, cultural and ethnic diversity.

  - **Fair Distribution** – Distribute awards equitably and in a timely manner covering all employees and contractors. Why? Safety contests and safety lucky hamper draw that reward only a few people or those events or activities reinforce the view that safety is a matter of chance or luck should be avoided.

  - **Union Culture** – Unions should be a partner in the design and roll-out of the incentive program. Why? Early union buy-in is key to selling the incentive program as a supporter of the incentive program rather than an opponent.

  - **Incentive Learning Curve** – Investigate and evaluate what other companies are doing, and review and consult the recent literature on successful programs on incentives. Design, implement and administer a cohesive plan, and then, give it time to see how that works; it could possibly be for the next two-three years. Revise and update the incentive program if or when required on the go!

- **Learn How To Recognize**: Many times, we fail to give recognition for a simple reason. How? It's not that the management does not want to, but, preferably, they do not know how to do it, what to say, when to say, when to stop, where to say it and how to say it. Here are some suggested steps for guidance:

  1. Be expeditious, sincere and timely on the recognition

  2. Call-out and thank the recipient(s) by name

  3. Be specific of the safe behavior being praised and rewarded

  4. State how the safe behavior added value to the company

  5. Explain how you felt about the safe behavior

  6. Share what recipients did to earn the recognition or award

  7. Take a photograph of the event

  8. Post photographs on safety bulletin boards, or publish them in safety newsletters

  9. Thank the person(s) again by name before concluding

- **Evaluate, Update Periodically, Stay Fresh:** You cannot press the go button, start an incentive program and then, walk away from it, and expect the program to grow and be run auto-pilot. How? Incentive Programs are to be adequately resourced, assessed, continuously refreshed and stewarded. A company can't expect to spread a safety culture if it doesn't back up its desire and actions without rewards, incentives and recognition programs which are upgraded with time.

Gift award is undoubtedly the catalyst. An integral part of a safety incentive program is to build teamwork, motivate and generate safe behaviors, promote safety awareness, create safety suggestions and recognizing employees for the right safe choices, behaviors, and habits. Simultaneously, do celebrate milestone successes as you progress on the journey down the path of safety excellence.

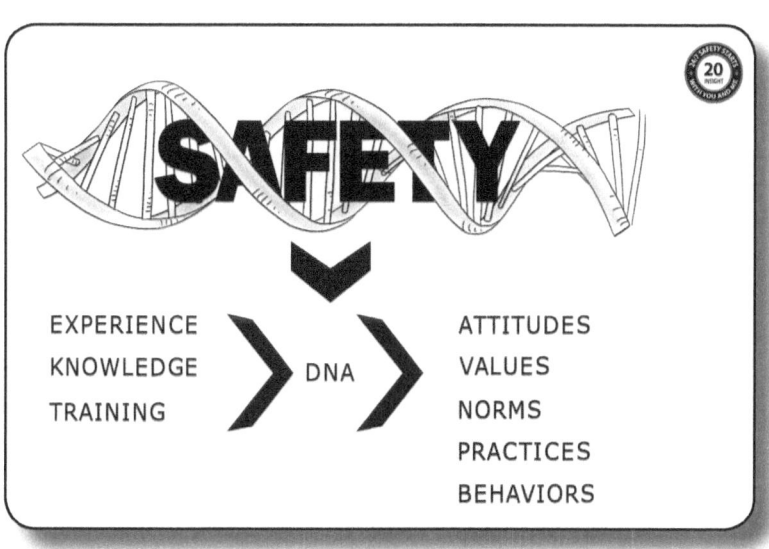

"No matter who you are, which company or organization you work for, where you work, where you are or what work you do, 24/7 SafetyDNA is relevant to you."

Insight 20

Culture, Style, Attributes And Results Matter; They Are The DNA Of Safety Leadership

For DNA leadership culture to design, nurture and activate in our profiles, we must first hybrid the SafetyDNA genetic code through our daily life leadership endurance and learnings. As human beings we have similarities: our blood is red, we have feelings, we know what pain is, we tear when we are sad or in suffering, and we laugh when we are happy. Why? We are 'sliced from the same loaf of bread.' However, the critical difference is we are 'toasted' differently based on family structure, culture, religion, race, the environment we grew up or the organizations we work. Some human elements may look similar or shared, but will never be all the same. Therefore, aspects of culture, styles, and attributes are not identical across people, businesses or companies.

Even though organizational safety culture or personality can be sensed or noticed across companies, one cannot assume it all lines up with the safety slogans or policies displayed at a company's reception front desk. Why? For all organizations to be safety cultured, it must bond cultures, styles, personalities, and attributes to deliver the desired safety performance.

- **Safety Leaders:** It is crucial for companies to identify, develop and station safety leaders across every level of the organization. Craig White, Select International (Art Of Work) said, **"Safety leaders set the standards of safe behavior within their companies. We would expect a Safety Leader to be someone who exhibits high SafetyDNA, but leadership is more than just managing one's**

safety behaviors. A real Safety Leader also motivates his or her co-workers to strive for minimal risk exposure."[23]

Let's now understand culture, style, and attributes a bit deeper:

- **Who Is A Safety Leader?** – A person who cares, who is relentless and passionate about core responsibilities to ensure the safety of the workforce. How? Acts to keep others and himself free from danger or injury through guidance, trust, respect, integrity, persuasion, and direction.

- **Who Can Be A Safety Leader?** – Any individual in the organization–if they so choose to be. It's anyone who steps up and volunteers to assume the role to serve. In short, it's must be a personal choice, usually, a choice driven by *24/7 SafetyDNA*!

- **How Does A Safety Leader Look Like?**–Individuals from various positions, companies and organization levels who do not influence others through power, status or authority. They demonstrate high *24/7 SafetyDNA* and relentlessly inspire co-workers to do the same. Safety Leaders continually review tolerance to risk and understand those small failures are signs that some things need fixing right away.

- **What Is Required To Be A Safety Leader?** – A person who puts people first at the heart of business or core of operations, and ensures work gets done, safely, on time, on schedule and within or under budget. One who never feels that the job is done, but relentlessly monitors and seeks ways to improve. He/she stays vigilant, and alert 24/7 to the possibility that something may go wrong.

- **What Does It Mean To Be A Safety Leader?** Although the position may appear burdensome and a time-consuming obligation which causes many to shy or stay away, one must realize that safety leaders take on no more significant share of the responsibilities and accountabilities than their co-workers.

The only difference is that safety leaders are more aware and tuned to their environments, and throughout the day, they are likely to be engaged or called upon by the management to coordinate safety tasks and actions.

- **Behaviors And Habits:** Different people of race, creed, religion, culture, personality, and intellect behave or react differently. Why? It's just the way people were hardwired; it is the reason why each of us is 'different' than the other. Therefore, each of us perceives and sees the world of safety through our perception determined and driven by our personal *24/7 SafetyDNA* genetic code. Everyone is unique, just as everyone's fingerprints are unique. Therefore, it's natural. It would result in different types of behaviors, actions, habits, reactions, and attitudes as each of us has our own personal DNA.

Hybrid of human beings SafetyDNA is imperative to trigger safe conscious compliance. Why? Being human beings, we are the most sophisticated machine on this planet, and we can influence our human body to serve and lead people without being driven and policed by social, corporate compulsion. As such, we need to do something beyond our human intellect. It's not going to be a process of artificial intelligence, but of human intelligence. Things that we as humans can control: attitudes, behavior, habits, personalities, choices, and actions. One such way is for 24/7 safety conscious compliance as depicted below.

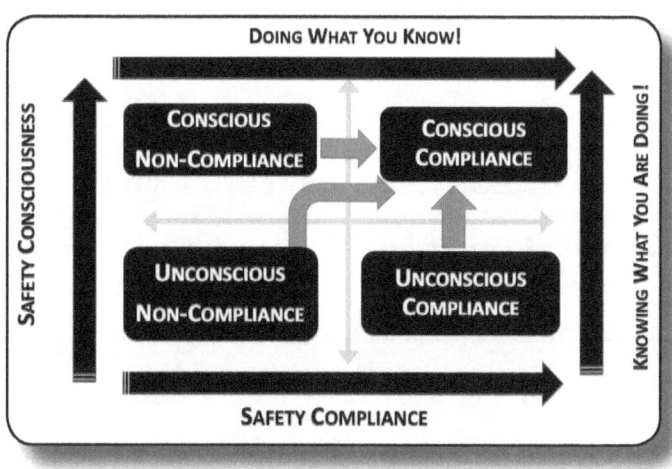

- **Safety Leadership:** People, materials, equipment, and worksites can change due to time, cost constraints, locality, environment, team composition, changes in procedures or weather conditions. But, your Safety*DNA* is always with you 24/7. How? It resides within our human body, and wherever you go, it goes with you. Thus, once your human behavior and personality had been designed, cultured and activated when an event or task puts you or your workers at-risk, you tend to be proactive to keep your co-workers and yourself safe regardless of the conditions, where you are or what you're doing.

What's the difference between Safety and *24/7 SafetyDNA*?

1. **Safety is focused on acquiring safety, risk, and operations integrity knowledge to manage lagging reactions**:

    - "We believe and know that safety is important to all of us."

    - "We do a lot every time we have an incident."

    - "We have safety and risk operations integrity systems in place to detect, reduce and manage our hazards."

    - "We work on safety issues when we find them or as they get reported."

2. *24/7 SafetyDNA* **predicts and shows actual safety behaviors, personality, habits, and choices of people with leading reactions**:

    - "Personal safety starts with the person!" That's you and me.

    - Focuses on personal traits, habits, behaviors, and attributes.

- *24/7 SafetyDNA* **Leadership Evolution:** Consolidation of leadership styles plus leadership attributes plus *24/7 SafetyDNA* finally equates to *24/7 SafetyDNA* leadership. The effect is everyone executes work safely:

    - "Even when no one is supervising or watching."

- "How everyone does business around here."

- "The way everyone executes and gets things done."

- "A pre-condition of employment and work."

The 5 phases of *24/7 SafetyDNA* Leadership Evolution on 'where we were, where we are and where we want to go' is shown on the graph and table below.

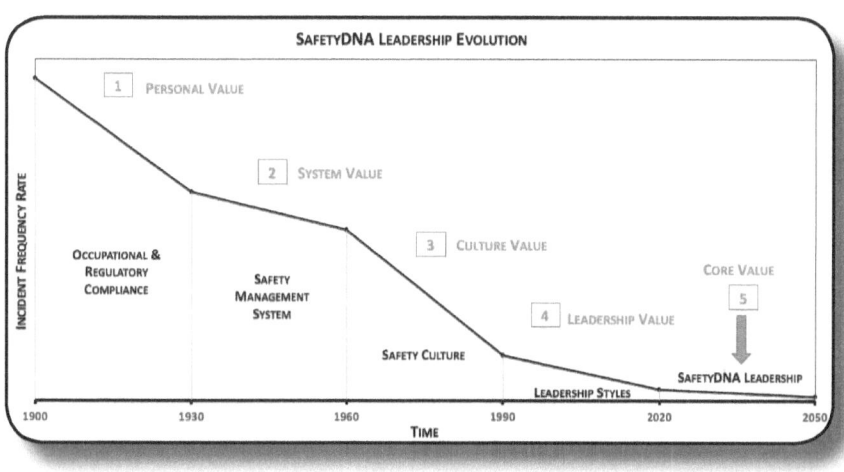

Management	People	Leadership		
Phase 1	Phase 2	Phase 3	Phase 4	Phase 5
Regulatory Compliance	Integrity Systems	Norms	Leadership Behaviour	Safety By Natural Instinct
Engineering	Risk Assessment	Beliefs	Leadership Best Practices	Pre-Condition Of Employment And Work
Legal Compliance	Goal Setting	Attitude	Caring, Compassion & Passion	Unspoken Norms
Technology	Rules & Procedures	Attributes	Compliance – License To Operate	Habitual Human Behaviour
Operating Procedures & Standards	Safety Knowledge	Accountability	Safe Behaviour Standards	Conscious Safety Competence
Administration	Auditing & Reviews	Responsibility	Trust And Respect	How We Do Things Around Here
PPE Compliance	Feedback Analysis	Working Together Rules	Integrity	Integrity Is What We Do When No One Is Watching
	Continuous Improvement			The Way We Really Get Things Done Here
	Managing Hazards			What We Do Even When No One Is Watching

Management	People	Leadership		
Phase 1	Phase 2	Phase 3	Phase 4	Phase 5
Why We Need To Do Something?	We Do Something As Its Required	We Need Workers To Comply And Show Behaviour	Individuals Taking Responsibility And Accountability	24/7 SafetyDNA Goes Everywhere You Go To Make It A Safe Workplace
Personal Value	System Value	Culture Value	Leadership Value	Core Value
Safety = Regulation	Safety = System	Safety = Culture	Safety = Leadership	Safety = DNA

"Only when the workforce executes the right safe choices for the right reasons, the right way, right time, every time even when no one is watching, then they are on their right 24/7 SafetyDNA journey."

Conclusion

It's A Journey, Not A Destination And Certainly Not A Magical One

Given the pace of change in the last 30 years, it is likely that the next 30 years we will see a multitude of new and creative safety, risk and integrity systems, safe choices and leadership practices with the emergence of advanced technologies and artificial intelligence to support and protect the complex 4.0 environment-friendly industries. Together with this, the associated challenges of hazards, risks, financial costs and implications for health, safety and environment issues and regulations would surface.

A fundamental challenge in this journey is how all of us are going to respond to future demographic, virtual reality and scientific and economic developments. Why? We live in a world where people continue to get hurt; lives get changed every day at workplaces due to a failure of individual responsibility or fault of personal safety leadership. **The challenge becomes more significant and complex as the rapidly evolving and robust business, technology, geopolitics, and demographic realities encroach on the status quo of our life.**

It's understood that changing and transforming to a culture of *24/7 SafetyDNA* leadership takes time and patience as you're dealing with people, and not machinery or equipment. It's not a change or upgrade of skill; it's *24/7 SafetyDNA* personality development through consolidation of styles, attitude, practices, behaviors, and habits to be incubated, as shown by the simple schematic below. The science behind is to assemble all the right ingredients, and you can whip up safety leadership culture in individuals driven by DNA.

SafetyDNA Leadership Culture Development

"It going to take a long time. Why? 'Safety is not a sprint to a destination; it's a marathon toward a journey.' No doubt about it!" In many corporations and industries, we work with people who've been around for many years in the industry who have seen safety programs, safety and integrity systems, and safety initiatives; not forgetting mandates, management styles and leadership practices come and go to make a change.

In the short-term, it's going to require perseverance, passion, relentless hard work and commitment on everyone's part – including corporate management. The role of corporate governance is crucial. Why? When ambiguities exist regarding precisely who should have, when should they have, why should they have and who have an influence on safety leadership culture; it indeed resides and starts with corporate leadership.

An insight with corporate management leadership is that the **barrier to success in the short-term is the belief that it is complicated to achieve this *24/7 SafetyDNA* leadership. The opposite view is that, in the long-term, it is more dangerous not to.** Investing in the safety and health of your most significant asset–people–is perhaps the most persuasive case any business leader can and must make. The payoff is enormous and priceless. It creates a positive attitude and behavior that sets the standard for safety and reduces incidents and hurts. For corporate leadership, what can be more rewarding than this?

After that, it is not a status or position – it is something to improve and grow into as conditions continuously change and evolve. Why? Whatever we lead, changes continually as the demands with leadership are always in flux. To be a successful and safe organization, all must have the courage and spirit to challenge the status quo from whatever and with whomever they lead.

Peter Drucker said, **"The best way to predict the future is to create it."**[24] Yes, creating, and after that, nurturing and activating a strong *24/7 SafetyDNA* leadership culture takes time and effort. But, we can start now. So, how do we progress on this journey?

❖ Be a legacy to 'transmit' this *24/7 SafetyDNA* on to the next generation to implant and activate a firm foundation; a continuity process upon which safety leaders of tomorrow will be able to build the road to safety excellence.

❖ Transfer safety knowledge to the next generation, what we have learned late or the painful way!

❖ Work together to develop new ways to establish and maintain a robust safety leadership culture such that employers take responsibilities seriously, the workforce is fully involved and committed, and at-risks are adequately mitigated or managed as the ultimate vision.

❖ Nurture full-blown *24/7 SafetyDNA* genetic code leadership evolution in every organizational program, every department and in every corporate initiative.

❖ Talk and breathe safety as a way of life. You not only talk about the core values, but you also embrace it, and with it, have all the required processes and systems to ensure that on your watch, no one gets hurt.

It's going to be a long and arduous journey. It's not going to be easy, but it's worth it and is an imperative one for human and corporate survival. **Safety is to be in everyone's DNA. It indeed requires an ingredient of *24/7 SafetyDNA* genetic code as a catalyst.** It's a journey, not a destination and certainly, not a magical one.

"Enjoy every second of your life, as time races by so much quicker than you think. Be safe, be happy, love genuinely and enjoy nature and life!"

Bibliography & References

1. **Page 32 – Definition of safety in English by Oxford Dictionaries**[1]

   https://en.oxforddictionaries.com/definition/safety2

2. **Page 42** – U.K. Health and Safety Commission definition of safety culture is as follows: "The product of individual and group values, attitudes, perceptions, competencies, and patterns of behavior that determine the commitment to, and the style and proficiency of, an organization's health and safety management." – HSC (Health And Safety Commission), 1993. Third report: organizing for safety. ACSNI Study Group on Human Factors. HMSO, London.[2]

3. **Page 50** – Entrenched assumptions, whether accurate or inaccurate, influence the behavior and attitudes of group members. Once ingrained, culture is highly resistant to change. – Building a Better Safety Vehicle, Leadership driven culture change at General Motors. By Steven I. Simon and Patrick Fraze, Page 38.[3]

4. **Page 53** – Anytime, workers perform anything in a company or organization, there is an element of risk involved; in fact, "is everything we do – from the moment we're born – carries an element of risk and his survival depends on how well he manages those risks." – Safety 24/7, Building An Incident-Free Culture; (2006), Gregory M. Anderson & Robert L. Lorber; Page 22.5[4]

5. **Page 59** – As said by Aristotle "we are what we repeatedly do; excellence, then, is not an act but a habit."[5]

6. **Page 75** – Paul O' Neill, CEO of Alcoa said "A great safety speech isn't about yelling orders and telling staff to improve safety and completely change their thinking or else. Instead, it's a unique opportunity a moment of time to motivate staff to work together and have open communications from the CEO down and unite for the common good of the group." – Alcoa CEO… The Greatest CEO Speech of the 20th Century? December 13, 2017.[6]

7. **Page 86** – "Leadership is not about titles, positions on organization flowcharts. It is about one life influencing another." –John Maxwell.[7]

8. **Page 89** – Mahatma Gandhi said it well – "A sign of a good leader is not how many followers you have, but how many leaders you create. – Mahatma Gandhi."[8]

9. **Page 103** – "If you wait for people to come to you, you'll only get small problems. You must go and find them. The big problems are where people don't realize they have one in the first place." (W. Edwards Deming).[9]

10. **Page 113** – Paul O'Neil, former CEO of Alcoa said it well with his Safety Policy: Executive Commitment; "I care about safety because I think it is a direct, tangible way to connect with human beings on a non-debatable goal that is truly important to every human being. Human beings are at the core of my definition of values."[10]

11. **Page 120** – The U.K. Health and Safety Executive defines safety culture as "the product of the individual and group values, attitudes, competencies, and patterns of behavior that determine the commitment to, and the style and proficiency of, an organization's health and safety programs." (1) A more

succinct definition suggested: "Safety culture is how the organization behaves when no one is watching." – U.K. Health and Safety Executive, Safety Culture: A Review of the Literature, HSL/2002/25, 2002.[11]

12. **Page 122** – Winston Churchill noted that "Character is what we do when no one is watching."[12]

13. **Page 123** – Henry Ford said; "Quality is doing it right when no one is watching."[13]

14. **Page 123** – As depicted in the Rick C. Torben's well-known iceberg schematic it shows the way an organization's safety is said, understood, functions and operates by "the way the organization got things done versus the way the organization really gets things done."[14]

15. **Page 131** – 5-steps, as outlined by the Ministry of Business, Innovation and Employment, in an article describe 5 – Steps "How To Approach Workers In A H&S Issue" business.govt.nz Worksafe New Zealand."[15]

16. **Page 134** – An excellent analysis sharing from Hebert William Heinrich. – 1920s.[16]

17. **Page 153** – According to Reason (1997), the components of a safety culture include: just, reporting, learning, informed and flexible cultures. Reason describes a Just Culture as an atmosphere of trust in which people are encouraged (even rewarded) for providing essential safety-related information, but in which they are also clear about where the line is drawn between acceptable and unacceptable behavior.[17]

18. **Page 160** – A learning is don't be like the Captain E.J. Smith of the Titanic, who is believed to have said this just prior to his fateful journey on board the Titanic in April 1912. "I will say that

I cannot imagine," he said, "any condition which could cause a ship to founder. I cannot conceive of any vital disaster happening to this vessel. Modern shipbuilding has gone beyond that."[18]

19. **Page 169** – Joseph Joubert said; "We must respect the past, and mistrust the present if we wish to provide the safety of the future."[19]

20. **Page 170** – After the worst industrial accident in the U.K. in modern times, the explosion on the Piper Alpha oil rig, Sir Brian Appleton stated that: "Safety is not an intellectual exercise to keep us in work. It is a matter of life and death. It is the sum of our contributions to safety management that determines whether the people we work with live or die."[20]

21. **Page 180** – Dr. Deming had the fundamental philosophy that data measurement and analysis were essential to attaining superior performance in every facet of business. A significant number of businesses do not know on how their business is performing, and more importantly, identifying ways to improve it. He advocated the believe that "In God we trust, the rest bring your data."[21]

22. **Page 185** – Herbert William Heinrich's shared take-home message encouraged employers to control hazards, not merely focus on worker behaviors, habits but one that reduces the number of near misses or hits.[22]

23. **Page 212** – Craig White, Select International (Art Of Work) says safety leaders set the standards of safe behavior within their companies. We would expect a Safety Leader to be someone who exhibits high SafetyDNA, but leadership is more than just managing one's safety behaviors. A true Safety Leader also motivates his or her co-workers to strive for minimal risk exposure."[23]

24. **Page 223** – Peter Drucker said it well "the best way to predict the future is to create it."[24]

25. **Page 241** – Deoxyribonucleic acid, more commonly known as DNA, is a complex molecule that contains all of the information necessary to build and maintain an organism. All living things have DNA within their cells. In fact, nearly every cell in a multicellular organism possesses the full set of DNAs required for that organism. However, DNA does more than specify the structure and function of living things—it also serves as the primary unit of heredity in organisms of all types. In other words, whenever organisms reproduce, a portion of their DNA is passed along to their offspring. This transmission of all or part of an organism's DNA helps ensure a certain level of continuity from one generation to the next, while still allowing for slight changes that contribute to the diversity of life. Introduction: What is DNA? | Learn Science at Scitable – Nature: [25]

https://www.nature.com/scitable/topicpage/introduction-what-is-dna-65799781

"Start strong so that you can end strong and keep moving in the forward safe chosen direction of your aspirations, dreams, and goals regardless of the speed of your train journey."

Closing Words

Life Is Like A Journey On A Train

Life is like a journey on a train...*with its stations*...*with changes of routes*...*and with accidents!*

At birth, we boarded the train and met our parents, and we believe they will always travel on our side.

However, at some station our parents will step down from the train, leaving us on this journey alone.

As time goes by, other people will board the train; and they will be significant i.e. our siblings, friends, children, and even the love of our life.

Many will step down and leave a permanent vacuum.

Others will go so unnoticed that we don't realize that they vacated their seats!

This train ride will be full of joy, sorrow, fantasy, expectations, hellos, goodbyes, and farewells.

Success consists of having a good relationship with all the passengers... requiring that we give the best of ourselves.

The mystery to everyone is:
We do not know at which station we ourselves will step down.

So, we must live in the best way—love, forgive, and offer the best of who we are.

It is important to do this because when the time comes for us to step down and leave our seat empty—we should leave behind beautiful memories for those who will continue to travel on the train of life.

I wish you a joyful journey for the coming year on the train of life. Reap success and give lots of love.

More importantly, thank God for the journey!

Lastly, I thank you for being one of the passengers on my train!

"If you learn about safety from other people's life-changing experiences, insights, observations, and thoughts, then you learn without a need to go through it yourself as it's shared by experience and not imagination."

About The Author: Personal Narrative

When I was just 14, my dad passed away. Being the eldest son in a family of six with the family responsibilities and unable to financially support by academics, my pre-university studies came to an abrupt stop. Thus, resigned to this fate at the age of 18, I deferred my tertiary education goals and embarked on a job search.

In the early 1970s, jobs were hard to come by in my small sleepy hometown of Bukit Mertajam, Penang, Malaysia. So, on New Year's Day 1973, I boarded a train and headed down south to our capital city of Kuala Lumpur, Selangor. I remember that day vividly, with the train ride. I wondered, '*Where would this 'journey of life' take me?*' I remember the advice from my mum prior to boarding the train; "Son, be safe. Take care of yourself while at work and during your travels."

They were sad, lonely and challenging moments for me. Why? My first time away from my hometown, my mum, brothers, sisters, schoolmates, friends, and relatives. Initially, I lived in Petaling Jaya, Selangor. I worked as a laboratory assistant with an Indian electronics company in Shah Alam, Selangor. This lasted ten months with a monthly salary of RM100. Eventually, after a series of job interviews, on Monday, November 19, 1973, I got a contract job with an American oil exploration company. It was an offshore job on an oil rig wildcat drilling off the east coast of Pahang, Malaysia. It was again anxious teenage moments for me. Why? Another of the many firsts. It was my first trip to the remote state of Pahang, Malaysia, the first helicopter travel, working offshore for the first time and the first time on an oil exploration drilling rig.

My job description ran the gamut: work schedule and work-hours, travel by train, road by taxi, air by helicopter, and the fortnight commutes were relentless. It was that first job on that oil rig that put in motion the rest of my oilfield career. My journey was covered with twists of fate and safety challenges–many heart-warming and heart-breaking. One that hits my heart and is entrenched in my mind was this incident at 10.55 a.m. on Monday, August 19, 1974. It was an incident that revamped my perspective about safety, or should I say, the one that gave me 'a safety wake-up call.'

"Three Teams A, B, and C had been rostered to work on the rig on a rotational cycle. Each team serves two weeks and then heads home for a week for shore break. I was the Team A Lead, and we were at the tail end of the fortnight offshore work cycle. The Team B Lead (Mustapha Chik, known as Mussy), who still had another week on the rig, requested if he could swap my place and go on shore break a week ahead as his wife was due for child delivery at any day and that I cover him for an additional week during his absence. Naturally, I said yes. Early morning, as scheduled, Team A with 15 souls on board departed from our exploration drilling rig via our helicopter toward Kuantan, Pahang but tragically, it did not reach the airbase as the aircraft had crashed about 50 miles from shore leaving no survivors."

What happened to that helicopter fight has made me to reflect further and deeper into life. 15 people from varying nationalities and races perished in a microsecond. Death didn't segregate; neither did it select them based on their religion, nationality or races. At the moment, they all belonged to one race, the human race, with no class or ethnic diversions. They all perished together. This twist of fate or 'divine intervention' forever changed my perception of safety. More so as I reflected on how short and unpredictable one's life could be. Personally, it had a profound impact with me, especially when I visited some of these families and witnessed the impact it had had emotionally, socially and financially. The ripple effect of this fatal incident continues to haunt me to this day. Even though I came to terms with this incident, I never forgot the consequence of 'failed' safety leadership. Why? An event such as this does cause one to reflect on why this incident could have occurred.

A question that keeps recurring till this very day; "If only; if only someone had intervened and stopped that aviation operation, we would have prevented it." Why do I say this? It was common knowledge that the helicopter operations had much safety, maintenance and operational issues which had resulted in numerous deferred or canceled crew changes. All operations performance indicators said that 'something was not right.' This is a big lesson about the simplicity of life that as long as we live, let us work for a better and safer life. It starts with leadership.

Ironically, no one took on the leadership role to STOP WORK. Not knowing why no one took on a leadership role actually turned out to be my greatest learning. How? I started doing things differently from others in terms of safety. Whenever I encountered or noticed something that's unsafe, I took action and did not walk away. Even though the helicopter operations were shutdown post this incident, pending completion of incident investigations, it was a post-incident reaction which had resulted in the irreversible loss of lives of 15 of our teammates.

I started my career in the oil and gas industry in the early 1970s; a period where the safety mindset was 'just meeting minimal safety standards and regulatory compliance.' It was an era when occupational health, safety, and regulatory compliance were in the infant stage of being formulated and rolled-out. I learned about safety on-the-job through co-workers, behavior, traits, practices, habits, observations, safety and risk assessments, on-the-job safety training and actual participation in incident investigations. Over the years, I worked for oil and gas companies initially as a contractor, and later as an employee in non-supervisory, supervisory, leadership, management, and senior management positions.

My passion in the present day is Safety Culture Leadership **DNA1**–[25] specifically, creating awareness, educating and sharing my safety insights. I believe that a resilient culture of safety ensures that everyone can go to work, do their jobs and return home safely to his or her loved ones. By holding this belief, we can mitigate incidents and prevent worker injuries and hurt at home, travel, and work.

My mother's safety message of Monday, January 1, 1973, continues to prolong in my mind and has deeply underscored my safety choices and actions throughout my 44 years in the oil and gas industry. I understood that safety, health, environment, security, and ethics are my core job descriptions.

Therefore, with retirement, working with the community and spending time with my family, I want to spread the message that **24/7 Safety Starts With You And Me** and no one else.

www.ingramcontent.com/pod-product-compliance
Lightning Source LLC
Chambersburg PA
CBHW030615220526
45463CB00004B/1296

9 7 8 1 6 4 8 5 0 6 3 4 5